Can One Person Make A Difference?

From the Bible-Teaching Ministry of

Charles R. Swindoll

INSIGHT *for* LIVING

Insight for Living's Bible teacher, Chuck Swindoll, has devoted his life to the clear, practical application of God's Word and His grace. A pastor at heart, Chuck has served as senior pastor to congregations in Texas, Massachusetts, and California. He currently leads Stonebriar Community Church in Frisco, Texas, but Chuck's listening audience extends far beyond a local church body. As a leading program in Christian broadcasting, *Insight for Living* airs in major Christian radio markets, through more than 2,100 outlets worldwide, in 16 languages, and to a growing webcast audience. Chuck's extensive writing ministry has also served the body of Christ worldwide, and his leadership as president and now chancellor of Dallas Theological Seminary has helped prepare and equip a new generation for ministry. Chuck and Cynthia, his partner in life and ministry, have four grown children and ten grandchildren.

Based on the outlines, charts, and transcripts of Charles R. Swindoll's sermons, in 1994, the Bible study guide text was co-authored by Bryce Klabunde, a graduate of Biola University and Dallas Theological Seminary. In 2002 this guide was revised and expanded by the creative ministries department of Insight for Living.

Editor in Chief:	**Editors:**
Cynthia Swindoll	Cheryl Gilmore
Study Guide Writer:	Tom Kimber
Bryce Klabunde	Amy LaFuria
	Glenda Schlahta
Senior Editor and Assistant Writer:	
Wendy Peterson	**Typesetter:**
	Bob Haskins
Editor and Assistant Writer:	
Marla Alupoaicei	

ISBN 1-57972-472-8
Cover design: Shawn Sturm
Cover etching: Luther Nailing His "Theses" to the Door of the Schloss-kirk at Wittenberg. Artist unknown.
Printed in the United States of America

CONTENTS

INTRODUCTION

All my life, I've heard that one person—just one single individual —can make a difference. The gritty Scottish reformer John Knox put it this way: "A man with God is always in the majority." Another person has suggested: "Never doubt the impact one person can make." Is that really true? Can one person be so significant that the world is altered in some way because of him or her?

To answer that question, I searched the corridors of church history and explored several of the back roads in the biblical record. Do you know what I found? Individuals from all walks of life— monks, kings, landowners, and peasants—who were committed to God made a difference in their world. It was thrilling to see! What's really exciting, though, is the thought that a few people reading this study could, in the next few years, be engaged in some life-changing venture, some leadership role, some particular niche in life that affects history. And to make that fact even more exciting, one of them could be *you!*

May this study broaden your horizons and clarify your vision of the amazing things God can do through your life. Yes . . . *your life!*

Charles R. Swindoll

PUTTING TRUTH
INTO ACTION

K nowledge apart from application falls short of God's desire for His children. He wants us to apply what we learn so that we will change and grow. This Bible study guide was prepared with these goals in mind. As you go through the following pages, we hope your desire to discover biblical truth will grow as your understanding of God's Word increases and that you will be encouraged to apply what you've learned.

To assist you in your study, we've included a section called ✑ **Living Insights** at the end of each lesson. These exercises and questions will challenge you to study further and to think of specific ways to put your discoveries into action.

Each Living Insights section is followed by ♟ **Small Group Insights.** These thought-provoking questions will help you to facilitate discussion of the important concepts and principles in the chapter and apply them to your life.

There are many ways to use this guide—in personal devotions, group studies, discussions with friends and family, and Sunday school classes. And, of course, it's an ideal study aid when you're listening to its corresponding *Insight for Living* radio series.

To benefit most from this Bible study guide, we encourage you to consider it a spiritual journal. That's why we've included space in the Living Insights for recording your thoughts and discoveries. We hope you'll return to those sections often for review and encouragement as you continue to grow in your walk with Christ.

Insight for Living

Can One Person Make A Difference?

A MIGHTY FORTRESS
IS OUR GOD

M usic," wrote Martin Luther, "is a gift and grace of God."[1] Through its majestic harmonies, it weaves the chords of courage and comfort. With its mighty crescendos, it plants determination and discipline into our souls. Of all the different, marvelous types of music, none makes me think deeper, stand taller, sing louder than the great hymn of the Reformation, "A Mighty Fortress Is Our God."

I love this grand old hymn. In a day when good, solid doctrine from the Scriptures is often lacking in our music, this great piece is dripping with biblical truth. Luther tugs on our heart's strings when he proclaims God as our helper and Jesus as the man on our side. It is *He* who will win our battle!

Anyone who knows Martin Luther's story knows his battle for truth. His name is a synonym for courage and determination—the same character qualities we need in our battles. In a day when warriors are scarce and surrender is more popular than firm convictions, this hymn brings us back to those needed reminders.

Read through the words slowly . . . thoughtfully. Even without the majestic chords building our anticipation, the message will stir your heart. Though Luther penned these lyrics almost five hundred years ago, it's amazing how up-to-date they really are! His struggles mirror our own. And his remarks about demonic assaults are as current as this morning's newspaper.

I often sing these words to myself or quote the lyrics when my courage needs undergirding. The song never fails to remind me where I need to go when I'm afraid or in whom I need to place my trust. My determination is strengthened when I sing, "We will not fear, for God hath willed His truth to triumph through us." God is our mighty fortress. Our bulwark. Our helper. We can trust Him!

Allow me to suggest to you a real faith-builder. In addition to

1. Kenneth W. Osbeck, *101 Hymn Stories* (Grand Rapids, Mich.: Kregel Publications, 1982), p. 14.

memorizing Scripture, commit this great piece of musical doctrine to memory. I guarantee it will strengthen your faith, because it will remind you of God's power and faithfulness. Perhaps you can sing it as a family before a meal or start your Bible study with it. However you weave it into your memory, never forget the scriptural truth on which it is built: "God is our refuge and strength, a very present help in trouble. Therefore we will not fear" (Ps. 46:1–2a).

Charles R. Swindoll

A Mighty Fortress Is Our God

The Lord Almighty is with us; the God of Jacob is our fortress. Ps. 46:7

1. A might-y for-tress is our God, A bul-wark nev-er fail - ing;
2. Did we in our own strength con-fide, Our striv-ing would be los - ing,
3. And tho this world, with dev-ils filled, Should threat-en to un-do us,
4. That word a-bove all earth-ly pow'rs, No thanks to them, a-bid - eth;

Our help-er He a-mid the flood Of mor-tal ills pre-vail - ing.
Were not the right man on our side, The man of God's own choos - ing.
We will not fear, for God hath willed His truth to tri-umph thru us.
The Spir-it and the gifts are ours Thru Him who with us sid - eth.

For still our an-cient foe Doth seek to work us woe—His craft and pow'r are
Dost ask who that may be? Christ Je-sus, it is He— Lord Sab-a-oth His
The prince of dark-ness grim, We trem-ble not for him— His rage we can en-
Let goods and kin-dred go, This mor-tal life al-so— The bod-y they may

great, And, armed with cru-el hate, On earth is not his e - qual.
name, From age to age the same, And He must win the bat - tle.
dure, For lo, his doom is sure: One lit-tle word shall fell him.
kill; God's truth a-bid-eth still: His king-dom is for-ev - er. A - men.

TEXT: Martin Luther; translated by Frederick H. Hedge; based on Psalm 46
MUSIC: Martin Luther

EIN' FESTE BURG
8.7.8.7.6.6.6.7.

Chapter 1

THE TRUTH THAT
SET US FREE

Selected Scriptures

The phone rings. On the line is your husband, calling to say his military assignment overseas has ended; he's on his way home.

In the hospital, your brother steadily recovers from life-threatening pneumonia.

You flip a switch and light rushes into a dark bedroom, chasing away your child's nighttime fears.

Three separate events. Yet a common thread is woven through them all: Each is the result of one person making a difference. Alexander Graham Bell made possible that phone call; Alexander Fleming developed the cure for your brother's illness, penicillin; and Thomas Edison invented the lightbulb illuminating your child's room.

Who can calculate the value of the contribution made by these visionaries and thousands of other men and women like them? Who can measure the amount of convenience afforded and the number of lives saved?

Scientists and inventors, however, aren't the only ones who can make the world a better place. You, too, can make a difference in the lives of those around you. You can be the one who brings people together or who heals the sick at heart or who shines the light of truth that scatters fear. You don't have to be educated or wealthy or even in good health. God can use you as you are, with the abilities He's already given you. With His help, *you* can make a difference!

To illustrate how God uses ordinary people, let's travel back in time to a period of history called the Reformation. The Reformation's heroes and battlefields may not be as recognizable as the American Revolution's George Washington and Valley Forge. Yet the soldiers who led this religious revolution from the 1300s to the 1500s made

1

a tremendous difference in what matters most to us—our under-standing of God, the Bible, and salvation.

John Wycliffe

Prior to the Reformation, a pall of spiritual ignorance shrouded the world. Piercing this thick gloom were three zealous and coura-geous men who lit a fire of truth that burned on throughout history. A sixteenth-century Bohemian Psalter depicts them in an illustra-tion with three panels. The first shows John Wycliffe striking the spark; the second, John Hus kindling the coals; and the third, Martin Luther brandishing the flaming torch.[1]

Let's go back, then, to the time the Reformation spark was first ignited in the small study of John Wycliffe.

In Wycliffe's day, religion was a polluted mixture of piety, poli-tics, and greed. Historian Stuart Garver explains that, during the late 1300s,

> a vast papal bureaucratic system was moved from Rome to Avignon in France, making bishops civil servants and ministers of State. The landed wealth of the clergy—estimated at about one-third of the nation's total—was not only tax exempt but im-mune to any legal action for its often cruel, if not criminal treatment of its poor tenants. . . .
> . . . Sunday and Holy Day Masses drew large crowds while priests and friars hawked their relics and indulgences as they mingled with the multitudes in the streets—having no higher motive than to in-crease the wealth of their already rich monasteries.[2]

Wycliffe, an Oxford-educated priest, was the first in a long line of Protestants—people who *protested* the corruptions in the estab-lished church. From his dimly lit study, he penned pamphlet after pamphlet, exposing the hypocrisies of the priesthood. His indict-ment was reminiscent of Jesus' rebuke of the Pharisees:

"They run fast, over land and sea, in great peril of

---

1. Harry Emerson Fosdick, ed., refers to this picture in *Great Voices of the Reformation* (New York, N.Y.: Random House, 1952), p. 3.

2. Stuart P. Garver, *Our Christian Heritage* (Hackensack, N.J.: Christ's Mission, 1973), p. 60.

body and soul, to secure rich benefices, but they will not go a mile to preach the Gospel, though men are running to hell for lack of the knowledge of God."[3] (compare Matt. 23:15)

As Wycliffe saw it, the priest's job was to communicate God's Word in a way the people could understand. However, not only were the priests falling short of their high calling; to make matters worse, the Bible was written in the dead language of Latin and chained to the pulpit—factors that made it accessible only to clergy. "Would to God," Wycliffe exclaimed,

"that every parish church . . . had a good Bible and good expositions on the Gospel, and that priests studied them well, and truly taught the Gospel and His commandments to the people! Then should good life prevail, and rest, and peace, and charity; sin and falseness should be put back—God bring this end to His people!"[4]

Driven by this vision, Wycliffe and his followers set out to translate the Latin Vulgate into English. Our Bibles today are distant cousins of Wycliffe's first English translation—a work that was completed in 1382 with this prophetic inscription written in the flyleaf:

"This Bible is translated and shall make possible Government of people, by people, for people."[5]

Almost five hundred years later, Abraham Lincoln borrowed those words for his Gettysburg Address as he spoke of "a new birth of freedom," proclaiming that "government of the people, by the people, for the people, shall not perish from the earth."[6]

However, no freedom awaited John Wycliffe. Because of his courageous stand against the church's hypocrisy, he was forbidden to preach and was stripped of his position as a professor at Oxford. Upon his death in 1384, he was called an "instrument of the devil,"

---

3. John Wycliffe, as quoted by Garver in *Our Christian Heritage*, p. 62.

4. Wycliffe, as quoted by Garver in *Our Christian Heritage*, p. 63.

5. Wycliffe, as quoted by Fosdick in *Great Voices of the Reformation*, p. 7.

6. Abraham Lincoln, as quoted in *Bartlett's Familiar Quotations*, 15th ed., rev. and enl., ed. Emily Morison Beck (Boston, Mass.: Little, Brown and Co., 1980), p. 523.

"author of schism," "sower of hatred," and "coiner of lies."[7] The religious hierarchy suppressed his writings and, in 1413, ordered his books burned. At the Council of Constance, the assembly declared John Wycliffe

> "to have been a notorious heretic, and excommunicates him and condemns his memory as one who died an obstinate heretic."[8]

They then ordered his body exhumed, burned, and thrown into the Swift River. But for all their censorial efforts, they could not silence his message or the truth of Scripture that was now in the hands of the people. One historian summed up the far-reaching impact of Wycliffe's life:

> "They burnt his bones to ashes and cast them into Swift, a neighboring brook running hard by. Thus this brook hath conveyed his ashes into Avon, Avon into Severn, Severn into the narrow seas, they into the main ocean. And thus the ashes of Wicliffe [sic] are the emblem of his doctrine, which now is dispersed the world over."[9]

John Wycliffe, the "Morning Star of the Reformation,"[10] had struck the first spark. John Hus, from Bohemia, would now take his place, kindling the coals until they glowed red hot.

John Hus

Ignited by Wycliffe's writings, John Hus burned with a passion to expose the religious charlatans and proclaim the truth of Scripture. Each time he preached at the Bethlehem Chapel in his home city of Prague, capacity crowds would sit in rapt attention, their hearts stirred by his boldness.

Stuart Garver gives us a taste of Huss' pointed oratory:

Confronted by representatives of the Pope sent to

7. Philip Schaff, *History of the Christian Church*, vol. 6, *The Middle Ages* by David S. Schaff, (Grand Rapids, Mich.: William B. Eerdmans Publishing Co., 1910), p. 324.

8. Schaff, *History of the Christian Church*, vol. 6, p. 325.

9. Fuller, as quoted by Schaff in *History of the Christian Church*, vol. 6, p. 325.

10. John D. Woodbridge, ed., *Great Leaders of the Christian Church* (Chicago, Ill.: Moody Press, 1988), p. 173.

silence Hus, the outspoken reformer declared: "Let it be understood that I call apostolic orders the teachings of the Apostles of Christ. When the pope's orders are in agreement with these I am ready to listen to them: *when they are contrary I refuse to obey them even if you were to kindle before my very eyes the fire in which my body was to be burned.*" [11]

Tragically, that last statement would prove to be prophetic. Summoned to appear before the Council of Constance, Hus was accused of "Wycliffism." When he refused to recant on the basis of no one's being able to show him from Scripture where his teachings were wrong, his enemies sentenced him to be burned at the stake. On that afternoon, July 6, 1415, three trumpeters riding black horses led him through crowded streets to his site of execution. He was lashed to the stake and smeared with pitch and oil. According to Garver, before the executioner lit the embers piled at Hus' feet he cried out this cryptic prophecy:

> "Today . . . you will roast a lean goose (the name Huss meant 'goose') but a hundred years from now you will hear a swan sing. Him you will leave un-roasted. No trap or net will catch him for you!" [12]

Within a few moments, smoke and flames swirled around him, and his voice was heard no more. Who would carry on the mission? Who was the "swan" that would sing and never be silenced?

Martin Luther

A century later in Germany, an unknown monk was waging a fierce, private battle of his own. To earn his salvation, Martin Luther was praying and fasting, piling on penance after penance, and working slavishly to attain God's favor. He once said, "If ever a monk got to heaven by monkery, I would have gotten there." [13] According to the church's standard of righteousness, he was impeccable. Yet

---

11. Garver, *Our Christian Heritage*, p. 51.

12. Garver, *Our Christian Heritage*, pp. 53–54.

13. Martin Luther, as quoted by Philip Schaff in *History of the Christian Church*, vol. 7, *Modern Christianity: The German Reformation*, 2d ed., rev. (Grand Rapids, Mich.: William B. Eerdmans Publishing Co., 1910), p. 116.

his conscience troubled him to despair. How could a sinful man like him stand under the scrutiny of a holy and exacting God?

Finally, his dark cell was flooded with spiritual light as one phrase from Romans 1:17 shone out: "But the righteous man shall live by faith." That beacon of truth led Luther to freedom. No longer was he bound by the demands of his works-based religion. He saw that righteousness is a gift that comes by faith in Christ alone.

In the years that followed, Luther would become the singing "swan" that challenged the false teachings of the church and proclaimed the good news of free salvation.[14] The flame of truth fit into Luther's hand as a blazing torch. Soon other reformers would light their torches from his, including:

- Ulrich Zwingli, the Swiss reformer who carried the Gospel to Zurich

- Philip Melanchthon, the gentle genius who honed Luther's theology and spread it throughout Germany

- John Calvin, the theologian some twenty-five years younger than Luther who built a center for reformation in Geneva

- John Knox, the tenacious clergyman influenced by Calvin who preserved Protestantism in Scotland

These fiery reformers are gone now, but their legacy continues as countless Christians continue to bear their message of justification by faith. And to think . . . this worldwide movement was begun by one man who ignited the spark, another who kindled the flame, and another who dared to brandish the torch of truth.

Concluding Comments

In the afterglow of the Reformation story, two facts remain impressed on our minds. First, *God used very human people to carry out the Reformation.* The reformers were courageous and brilliant, but they were not superhuman. Their passion for truth sometimes became an angry tempest within their souls. Luther once admitted,

"I never work better . . . than when I am inspired of anger; when I am angry, I can write, pray and

---

14. In the next chapter, we'll take a deeper look into Luther's discovery and the ways he confronted the teachings of the church.

preach well, for then my whole temperament is quickened, my understanding sharpened, and my mundane vexations and temptations depart."[15]

Do you get impassioned about your faith, even to the point of extreme? Do people sometimes consider you a fanatic? Welcome to the club of the reformers—you fit right in! Today the torch is still carried by people who get emotional about the Gospel.

Second, *the grassroots work of the Reformation was done by ordinary people, the laity.* Historian Harry Emerson Fosdick locates the ultimate power of the Reformation—within the hearts of the people:

> The Luthers and Calvins and kings could have done nothing, had there not been widespread among the people both indignant rebellion against the abuses of the Roman church and zealous piety, seeking a religion of personal experience, vital power and intelligent credibility.[16]

It is within our hearts that the Reformation spirit lives on. The just *shall* live by faith. Salvation *is* free in Christ. We *can* make a difference in our world, as we and thousands like us carry the flame and pass it on to generations to come.

 Living Insights

The Bible continues to be the world's number one best-selling English-language book. We see Bibles everywhere—in hotel rooms, in hospitals, and in bookstores. You probably own several specially tailored versions: a pocket Bible, a study Bible, a children's Bible, a coffee-table Bible, an easy-to-read Bible, a witnessing Bible, an heirloom Bible.

However, imagine a time prior to the Reformation when there was only one Bible in town. And it was written in a language you didn't understand and chained to a pulpit you couldn't go near. To keep you compliant and ignorant, elitist clergy dispensed dogma according to their greedy purposes. Of course, you had no way to

---

15. Luther, as quoted by Garver in *Our Christian Heritage*, p. 31.

16. Fosdick, ed., *Great Voices of the Reformation*, pp. xxix–xxx.

verify their teaching, so you were forced to believe whatever they said for fear of losing your soul.

Then came the reformers who, at the cost of their lives, gave you a Bible you could understand and who shone the light of the true Gospel into your darkness. How grateful you would be! How free!

Do you sometimes take your Bible for granted—and the price that others have paid for you to own one? Has the Bible become so commonplace that it has lost its precious value? How does the story of the Reformation change your attitude toward Scripture?

_____

_____

_____

Small Group Insights

1. What have you learned from this chapter about the great leaders of the Reformation? How did God use them to bring about change?

   _____

   _____

   _____

2. Discuss the events leading up to the Reformation. How would you characterize the political and religious climate of the times? How did this affect the people spiritually?

   _____

   _____

   _____

3. How would you characterize the church today? What are some of our modern struggles? Your personal struggles?

   _____

   _____

   _____

4. Name some leaders who are standing strong for the truth in your country, community, and church. What characteristics do these people possess? How is God working in their lives?

_____

_____

_____

5. How can you demonstrate your faith to others around you? Name three tangible ways you can show faith and love this week.

_____

_____

_____

Chapter 2

A MONK, A DOOR, A WAR, A HYMN

Selected Scriptures

Walking the hallways of the Capitol in Washington, D.C., is, in itself, a course in U.S. history. The larger-than-life portraits of past presidents speak silently about their times and their unique roles in shaping the nation. Displayed here are the country's foremost difference-makers: George Washington, Thomas Jefferson, James Madison, and many others whose presence lingers in the broad corridors.

A similar collection of portraits lines the halls of Hebrews 11. These influential men and women, though, are not exhibited because of their leadership skills as much as for their courageous faith. Here are paintings of Abel . . . Enoch . . . Noah . . . Abraham. On and on the hallway stretches—Isaac . . . Jacob . . . Joseph . . . Moses . . . Rahab . . .

So long is the corridor that the writer is unable to describe all the pictures it contains:

> And what more shall I say? For time will fail me
> if I tell of Gideon, Barak, Samson, Jephthah, of David
> and Samuel and the prophets . . . (v. 32)

Even the prophets don't end the list! The hall of faith extends throughout church history—yes, we could continue the collection with William Tyndale, John Wesley, George Whitefield, and others.

In the previous chapter, we studied several faithful men from the Reformation era. Time failed us, though, to tell the whole story of the greatest difference-maker of that period, Martin Luther. Let's pause for a while at his portrait and draw courage from his example of faith.

A Monk

The son of a poor German miner, Martin Luther was born on November 10, 1483, one hour before midnight—appropriately, the eleventh hour. While his father worked the mines, his mother toiled in the forests, hauling wood on her back. Luther once said that his parents "worked their flesh off their bones" raising him and his six younger brothers and sisters.[1]

Concerning Luther's growing-up years, historian Philip Schaff sketches a cheerless picture:

> Luther had a hard youth, without sunny memories, and was brought up under stern discipline. His mother chastised him, for stealing a paltry nut, till the blood came; and his father once flogged him so severely that he fled away and bore him a temporary grudge. . . . He was taught at home to pray to God and the saints, to revere the church and the priests, and was told frightful stories about the devil and witches which haunted his imagination all his life.[2]

Religion, for young Luther, was just another tributary of the stern discipline and fearful superstitions that coursed through his life. Historian Harry Emerson Fosdick describes Luther's dreadful impression of Christianity:

> The appeal to fear, powerfully used in the church, struck terror into his youthful conscience, and he never forgot the stained-glass window in the parish church of Mansfeld where Jesus, with frowning face, seated on a rainbow with sword in hand, threatened judgment to come. How could he save his soul?— that question obsessed him.[3]

One day, Luther came face-to-face with his fears of devils and a vengeful God when a violent storm overtook him. The thunder and lightning so frightened him, according to Schaff, that "he fell to the earth and tremblingly exclaimed: 'Help, beloved Saint Anna! I will become a monk.'"[4] To escape the tempest of God's judgment, Luther flung himself upon the altar of religious duty. But his frowning God of judgment was to him no friend—only a fault-finding parent whom he must constantly appease.

---

1. Martin Luther, as quoted by Philip Schaff in History of the Christian Church, vol. 7, Modern Christianity: The German Reformation, 2d ed., rev. (Grand Rapids, Mich.: William B. Eerdmans Publishing Co., 1910), p. 106.

2. Schaff, History of the Christian Church, vol. 7, p. 108.

3. Harry Emerson Fosdick, ed., Great Voices of the Reformation (New York, N.Y.: Random House, 1952), p. xxiv.

4. Schaff, History of the Christian Church, vol. 7, p. 112.

The church was no friend either. It should have been a shelter, offering comfort and direction for earnest pilgrims like himself. Instead, corruption had all but crumbled its ornately carved facade. Luther observed three contributing factors:

- *Hypocrisy and moral debauchery among the professional clergy.* Erasmus, a priest and contemporary of Luther, lamented the deplorable behavior of his fellow clergymen:

  "There are priests now in vast numbers, enormous herds of them, seculars and regulars, and it is notorious that very few of them are chaste. The great proportion fall into lust and incest, and open profligacy."[5]

- *Biblical illiteracy among the people.* Commoners had little access to a Bible in their own language, and the teachers who could decipher the old Latin version sullied the Scripture with their ineptitude. Listen to Erasmus' blistering indictment of the theologians of his day:

  "Theology itself I reverence and always have reverenced. I am speaking merely of the theologastrics of our time, whose brains are the rottenest, intellects the dullest, doctrines the thorniest, manners the brutalest, life the foulest, speech the spitefulest, hearts the blackest that I have ever encountered in the world."[6]

- *Unabashed materialism among the clergy.* The final worm in the woodwork of the church was greed. According to one sixteenth-century observer, ministers were constantly grubbing for money:

  "I see that we can scarcely get anything from Christ's ministers except for money; at baptism money, at bishoping money, at marriage money, for confession money—no, not extreme unction without money! They ring no bells without money, no burial in the church without money; so that it seemeth that Paradise is shut up from them that have no money."[7]

Luther longed to right the many wrongs in the Roman church,

5. Erasmus, as quoted by Fosdick in *Great Voices of the Reformation*, p. xxi.

6. Erasmus, as quoted by Fosdick in *Great Voices of the Reformation*, p. xx.

7. Juan de Valdez, as quoted by Fosdick in *Great Voices of the Reformation*, p. xvi.

yet he never thought of himself as a rebel. As far as he was concerned, the church still taught the way of salvation—personal
merit—and he determined to follow that path to the gates of
heaven. Fosdick writes,

> He became the embodiment of monastic piety. He
> fasted, scourged himself, piled penance on penance,
> confessed and sought absolution for every slightest
> peccadillo he could accuse himself of, until he was
> ordered to stop confession until he had done some-
> thing wrong enough to be worth confessing. Luther
> wrote later (1518) that no pen could describe his
> mental torture. He was struggling to achieve his
> soul's salvation by "good works," and he was getting
> nowhere.[8]

Frustrated and disillusioned, Luther found himself drowning in
a churning sea of legalism. Then an older friend and mentor, Johannes
von Staupitz, threw him a line of hope in the form of some wise
counsel. According to Philip Schaff,

> He directed him from his sins to the merits of Christ,
> from the law to the cross, from works to faith, from
> scholasticism to the study of the Scriptures.[9]

And it was through Luther's study of Scriptures, particularly
Paul's letter to the Romans, that God drew him out of the abyss
and set him on the solid ground of faith in Christ alone. These
words of Paul captivated the young monk:

> For I am not ashamed of the gospel, for it is the
> power of God for salvation to everyone who be-
> lieves, to the Jew first and also to the Greek. For in
> it the righteousness of God is revealed from faith to
> faith; as it is written, "But the righteous man shall
> live by faith." (Rom. 1:16–17)

Schaff gives us a window into Luther's mind as he brooded over
these verses:

> He pondered day and night over the meaning of "the

---

8. Fosdick, *Great Voices of the Reformation*, pp. xxiv–xxv.
9. Schaff, *History of the Christian Church*, vol. 7, p. 119.

righteousness of God" (Rom. 1:17), and thought that it is the righteous punishment of sinners; but toward the close of his convent life he came to the conclusion that it is the righteousness which God freely gives in Christ to those who believe in him. Righteousness is not to be acquired by man through his own exertions and merits; it is complete and perfect in Christ, and all the sinner has to do is to accept it from Him as a free gift.[10]

As Luther studied further, verses in Romans 3 and 4 seemed to leap off the page and into his heart.

> But now apart from the Law the righteousness of God has been manifested, being witnessed by the Law and the Prophets, even the righteousness of God through faith in Jesus Christ for all those who believe; for there is no distinction; for all have sinned and fall short of the glory of God, being justified as a gift by His grace through the redemption which is in Christ Jesus. (3:21–24)

> Now to the one who works, his wage is not credited as a favor, but as what is due. But to the one who does not work, but believes in Him who justifies the ungodly, his faith is credited as righteousness. (4:4–5)

At long last, the truth of God's justification of sinners broke through the clouds that overshadowed Luther's life. Schaff explains the magnificent doctrine that overcame him:

> Justification is that judicial act of God whereby he acquits the sinner of guilt and clothes him with the righteousness of Christ on the sole condition of personal faith.[11]

No amount of good works can earn Christ's righteousness—it is a gift received by faith. Only then, once received, does it flow out to others in the form of good works. For Luther, the dawning of this truth in his mind was a Damascus Road experience. A

10. Schaff, *History of the Christian Church*, vol. 7, p. 122.
11. Schaff, *History of the Christian Church*, vol. 7, p. 122.

Pharisee of Pharisees, he became wholly converted and, like Paul, would step into the world's arena as one of history's greatest champions of grace.

A Door

With the fire of God's truth burning in his soul, Luther was bound to clash with the hypocritical false teachers of his day. The first sparks flew over the practice of selling indulgences—letters from the pope conferring spiritual merit that would release the owners or their dead loved ones from purgatorial suffering. Papal representatives traveled the countryside in circus style, hawking these spiritual favors.

Luther, who had received remission of sin as a free gift from God, could not stand by and watch these religious charlatans extort the people. So on October 31, 1517, at twelve o'clock, he nailed his Ninety-five Theses on the subject of indulgences to the door of the castle-church in Wittenberg, unwittingly launching the Reformation.

He chose that day, the eve of All Saints' Day, because he knew that people from all over the region would visit the church during the festival. It was common practice for notices to be posted on the church door; Luther had done nothing unusual. Yet his Theses expressed, to borrow Victor Hugo's words, "an idea whose time [had] come."[12] At first no one challenged Luther, but as the papers were copied and distributed throughout the country, the spark grew into a blaze that neither the world nor the pope could ignore.

A War

Pope Leo X tried to dismiss the ruckus as a "mere squabble of envious monks" and derided Luther by saying, "It is a drunken German who wrote the Theses; when sober he will change his mind."[13] But Luther was neither drunk nor willing to change his mind. He stood firm as the church pummeled him with artillery fire in debates and councils—called "diets." At the famous diet in the city of Worms, Luther was called upon to renounce his

---

12. Victor Hugo, as quoted in Bartlett's Familiar Quotations, 15th ed., rev. and enl., ed. Emily Morison Beck (Boston, Mass.: Little, Brown and Co., 1980), p. 491.

13. As quoted by Schaff in History of the Christian Church, vol. 7, p. 171.

"heretical" theology. Surrounded by his fuming enemies, he announced in a clear voice:

> "I must be bound by those Scriptures which have
> been brought forward by me; yes, my conscience has
> been taken captive by these words of God. I cannot
> revoke anything, nor do I wish to; since to go against
> one's conscience is neither safe nor right: here I
> stand, I cannot do otherwise. God help me. Amen."[14]

A Hymn

For years, the fight dragged on. Luther was called "an ignorant and blasphemous arch-heretic"[15] and pictured holding hands with the devil. He was despised, threatened, and excommunicated. Yet the Gospel message never wavered on his lips as the cry of the Reformation sounded forth: *sola fide*, "faith alone."

Luther often expressed his faith in God by writing hymns. Of his thirty-seven hymns, his flagship was "A Mighty Fortress Is Our God," the victory anthem of the Reformation. Based on Psalm 46, this song of courageous faith declares the reformer's confidence in God, His unassailable refuge. The arrows of men may fly all around, depressions and doubts may rage within, but God's strength is sure, and Christ is our champion.

> A mighty fortress is our God,
> A bulwark never failing;
> Our helper He amid the flood
> Of mortal ills prevailing.
> For still our ancient foe
> Doth seek to work us woe—
> His craft and pow'r are great,
> And, armed with cruel hate,
> On earth is not his equal.
>
> Did we in our own strength confide,
> Our striving would be losing,
> Were not the right man on our side,
> The man of God's own choosing.

14. Luther, as quoted by Fosdick in *Great Voices of the Reformation*, p. 80.
15. Schaff, *History of the Christian Church*, vol. 7, p. 171.

Dost ask who that may be?
Christ Jesus, it is He—
Lord Sabaoth His name,
From age to age the same,
And He must win the battle.[16]

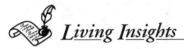 *Living Insights*

The bane of a works-based salvation is never knowing whether you've done enough to compensate for your sins and balance the spiritual ledger. According to biographer Roland Bainton, Martin Luther never found peace of mind during his days as a pious monk:

> He fasted, sometimes three days on end without a crumb. . . . He laid upon himself vigils and prayers in excess of those stipulated by the rule. He cast off the blankets permitted him and well-nigh froze himself to death. At times he was proud of his sanctity and would say, "I have done nothing wrong today." Then misgivings would arise. "Have you fasted enough? Are you poor enough?"[17]

Do similar misgivings concerning your salvation ever haunt you? Do you wonder whether you've given enough of yourself to God, said enough prayers, or sacrificed enough pleasure to earn His favor? If so, explore those worries a little deeper. How do they affect your attitude toward God?

_____

_____

_____

_____

_____

_____

16. Martin Luther, trans. Frederick H. Hedge, "A Mighty Fortress Is Our God," in *Hymns for the Family of God* (Nashville, Tenn.: Paragon Associates, 1976), no. 118.

17. Roland H. Bainton, *Here I Stand: A Life of Martin Luther* (New York, N.Y.: Abingdon-Cokesbury Press, 1950), p. 45.

On the debit side, do you sometimes fear that you've charged so much sin against your account that there is no hope of forgiveness? How does this impact your perception of God?

_____

_____

_____

_____

For years, Luther trembled before the Lord, even as you may today. Then the light of God's grace warmed his heart. Here is Luther's own account of how he met that grace:

> "I greatly longed to understand Paul's Epistle to the Romans and nothing stood in the way but that one expression, 'the justice of God,' because I took it to mean that justice whereby God is just and deals justly in punishing the unjust. My situation was that, although an impeccable monk, I stood before God as a sinner troubled in conscience, and I had no confidence that my merit would assuage him. Therefore I did not love a just and angry God, but rather hated and murmured against him. Yet I clung to the dear Paul and had a great yearning to know what he meant.
>
> "Night and day I pondered until I saw the connection between the justice of God and the statement that 'the just shall live by his faith.' Then I grasped that the justice of God is that righteousness by which through grace and sheer mercy God justifies us through faith. Thereupon I felt myself to be reborn and to have gone through open doors into paradise. The whole of Scripture took on a new meaning, and whereas before the 'justice of God' had filled me with hate, now it became to me inexpressibly sweet in greater love. This passage of Paul became to me a gate to heaven. . . .
>
> "If you have a true faith that Christ is your Saviour, then at once you have a gracious God, for faith leads you in and opens up God's heart and will,

that you should see pure grace and overflowing love. This it is to behold God in faith that you should look upon his fatherly, friendly heart, in which there is no anger nor ungraciousness."[18]

Small Group Insights

1. How did Martin Luther's upbringing and background prepare him to fulfill God's plan for his life?

_____

_____

_____

2. In what ways did Martin Luther try to "earn his way" to heaven? How do non-Christians often do this? Christians?

_____

_____

_____

3. How have you encountered legalism and hard-heartedness in your Christian life? Where were you? How did you deal with those who did not dispense God's grace?

_____

_____

_____

4. How is God's grace manifested in your life? What steps can you take this week to demonstrate grace to others?

_____

_____

_____

18. Luther, as quoted by Bainton in _Here I Stand_, p. 65.

Chapter 3
BEING A CHURCH THAT MAKES A DIFFERENCE
Revelation 2–3

You can't judge a book by its cover. That's a phrase we've all heard before. It simply means you can't evaluate people by externals—the clothes they wear, their appearance, or their size. Beneath Cinderella's ragged and sooty cover was a princess waiting to dazzle her prince. And young David—who would have imagined that this young shepherd would kill a giant with one well-placed stone?

What's true of people is also true of churches. The small church building on the corner with peeling paint and cardboard taped over broken windows may house a group of vibrant Christians who are making a real difference in their community. Of course, the opposite is also true. Down the street there could be a large, impressively ornate church that feels like a mortuary inside. No, you can't tell a book by its cover . . . nor a church by its building.

What does it take for our churches to make a difference for Christ? To find the answer, we must first forget about externals. Things like financial health and staff size are the "outward appearance" of a church, but "the Lord looks at the heart" (1 Sam. 16:7b). To discover the traits of an effective church, we have to examine what's on the inside. Fortunately, Jesus Himself shows us what to look for.

Seven Letters to Seven Churches

In Revelation 2 and 3, John records seven letters that Christ dictated to him and addressed to seven first-century churches in Asia. It's as if Jesus has made an inspection tour of the troops, and the letters represent His evaluation and recommendations. These are rare and precious documents. Only this once in history has the Head of the church revealed His opinions about a local body. Possibly, He chose these churches because they were located at strategic cultural crossroads and had the most potential for making a difference in their day.

He sends the letters to the churches via the "angel" of each church. The word *aggelos* in Greek could mean "messenger." It could also refer to the leader of the assembly or a literal guardian angel. In any case, the letters are sent, and each includes a personal statement— for example, "I know your deeds" (2:2)—an exhortation, and a promise. Jesus, the One who sees and knows all, doesn't hold back any inside facts. "All the churches will know," announces the Savior, "that I am He who searches the minds and hearts" (2:23b).

The churches He selects for His searching evaluation are:

- The church in Ephesus (2:1–7).

- The church in Smyrna (2:8–11).

- The church in Pergamum (2:12–17).

- The church in Thyatira (2:18–29).

- The church in Sardis (3:1–6).

- The church in Philadelphia (3:7–13).

- The church in Laodicea (3:14–22).

What if a messenger from God winged down from heaven and delivered a letter from Christ to your church? What things do you think He would commend? What would He criticize? Tragically, for two of the churches in Asia—the ones in Sardis and Laodicea— Christ issues no stars of praise. But to the other five, He points out several positives. By focusing on Christ's statements of approval, we will find five difference-making qualities that our churches can emulate.

Characteristics of Churches That Make a Difference

The first church Christ commends was once Paul's ministry headquarters in Asia—the church at Ephesus.

Ephesus: Persevering Commitment to Orthodoxy

"To the angel of the church in Ephesus write:
The One who holds the seven stars in His right hand, the One who walks among the seven golden lampstands, says this: 'I know your deeds and your toil and perseverance, and that you cannot tolerate evil men, and you put to the test those who call themselves apostles, and they are not, and you found them to be false; and you have perseverance and

21

have endured for My name's sake, and have not grown weary.'" (2:1-3)

Let's highlight the Ephesians' "deeds" that caused our all-seeing Lord to stand up and applaud:

- Hard work—"toil"

- Steadfastness under pressure—"perseverance"

- Discernment—"you put to the test those who call themselves apostles"

- Endurance—"have endured for My name's sake, and have not grown weary"

Wrapped into one bundle, these qualities show *a persevering commitment to orthodoxy.* The Ephesian church was able to think clearly, distinguish truth from error, and pursue righteousness. Paul had given them a solid theological ballast that stabilized them in seas of persecution and kept them on course when the winds of false teaching started to blow.

Today, as waves of immorality and injustice pound our society, the church must equip itself with an equally strong ballast of orthodoxy. By *orthodoxy* we mean the long-standing, traditional teachings of Scripture: the facts about God, Christ, and humanity; the truth about sin, salvation, and our future hope. Where else can we find these spiritual anchors? Certainly not on the political platform or in the arts. Only the church is equipped to navigate the moral storms facing society in the years to come.

Smyrna: Unswerving Courage through Suffering

The second assembly Christ writes to is Smyrna, "the crown of Asia."[1]

"And to the angel of the church in Smyrna write: The first and the last, who was dead, and has come to life, says this: 'I know your tribulation and your poverty (but you are rich), and the blasphemy by those who say they are Jews and are not, but are a synagogue of Satan. Do not fear what you are about

1. William Barclay, *The Revelation of John,* vol. 1, rev. ed., The Daily Study Bible Series (Philadelphia, Pa.: Westminster Press, 1976), p. 73.

to suffer. Behold, the devil is about to cast some of you into prison, so that you will be tested, and you will have tribulation for ten days. Be faithful until death, and I will give you the crown of life.'" (vv. 8–10)

The inner quality written on the pages of these believers' lives is *unswerving courage through suffering*. Jesus said, "I *know* your tribulation." He too had borne the weight of suffering. Death had sought Him and silenced Him, but only temporarily.

The Greek word for "tribulation," *thlipsis*, means "pressure." According to commentator William Barclay,

> In classical Greek it is always used in its literal sense. It is, for instance, used of a man who was tortured to death by being slowly crushed by a great boulder laid upon him.[2]

Under the oppressive weight of persecution, the believers in Smyrna faced imprisonment and even death.[3] But Jesus said, "Do not fear." They would have waiting for them a priceless, Christ-given crown—a crown not of glimmering rubies and emeralds but of eternal life.

Stones of imprisonment and death may not hang over us, but we do experience the weight of antagonism, cynicism, and ridicule. And in the coming days, the weight will press down more and more heavily. "Do not fear," says Christ. Fear keeps us cloistered behind ecclesiastical walls. It puts a gag in our mouths and binds us with the cords of reluctance. Instead of being afraid, we are to stand tall and draw courage from the One who has gone before and calls us to eternal life.

2. William Barclay, *Letters to the Seven Churches* (1957; reprint, London, England: SCM Press, 1958), p. 40.

3. "About sixty years later (c. 156), Polycarp was burned alive at the age of eighty-six as 'the twelfth martyr in Smyrna.' . . . His words have echoed through the ages: 'Eighty-six years have I served Christ, and he has never done me wrong. How can I blaspheme my King who saved me?'" As quoted by Alan F. Johnson in *The Expositor's Bible Commentary*, ed. Frank E. Gaebelein (Grand Rapids, Mich.: Zondervan Publishing House, Regency Reference Library, 1981), vol. 12, p. 437.

Pergamum: Uncompromising Witness That Remains on the Cutting Edge

Continuing, Jesus addresses the believers in Pergamum.

> "And to the angel of the church in Pergamum write:
> The One who has the sharp two-edged sword says this: 'I know where you dwell, where Satan's throne is; and you hold fast My name, and did not deny My faith even in the days of Antipas, My witness, My faithful one, who was killed among you, where Satan dwells.'" (vv. 12–13)

Pergamum was the capital city and cultural center of Asia, with a library rivaling the renowned library of Alexandria. Also, according to Barclay,

> Pergamum . . . was the centre of Caesar worship for the province. . . .
> . . . Undoubtedly that is why Pergamum was Satan's seat; it was the place where men were required on pain of death to take the name of Lord and give it to Caesar instead of to Christ; and to a Christian there could be nothing more Satanic than that.[4]

In addition to this, above the lofty city an imposing altar to Zeus was situated in front of the Temple of Athena. "It stood on a projecting ledge of rock and looked exactly like a great throne on the hillside. All day it smoked with the smoke of sacrifices offered to Zeus," writes Barclay.[5]

They were indeed living "where Satan's throne is." But with Christ's "sharp two-edged sword" of truth, they were slashing a hole in Satan's kingdom. The quality we see in this church is *an uncompromising witness that remains on the cutting edge*.

The church that makes a difference in our time must also be willing to stand firm in the thick of battle and press forward to win back those captured by the evil one. Every city has a place where "Satan's throne" is. Don't retreat from it. Stay where the action is.

---

4. Barclay, *The Revelation of John*, vol. 1, p. 90.
5. Barclay, *The Revelation of John*, vol. 1, p. 89.

Keep in touch with the lost world. If we hope to pierce the kingdom of darkness, we must remain on the cutting edge.

Thyatira: Increasing Zeal for Things Eternal

Next on Christ's list is the church at Thyatira.

> "And to the angel of the church in Thyatira write: The Son of God, who has eyes like a flame of fire, and His feet are like burnished bronze, says this: 'I know your deeds, and your love and faith and service and perseverance, and that your deeds of late are greater than at first.'" (vv. 18–19)

As with the Ephesian believers, the Lord commends those in Thyatira for their deeds, namely the ones done in love, faith, service, and perseverance. And, Christ points out, their deeds were becoming greater and greater. There was no slowing down these Christians! They were on the move, cruising forward, always looking ahead. We might say that they had an *increasing zeal for things eternal*.

Churches tend to lose momentum when their members are constantly looking in the rearview mirror at past glories. One person has said: "When you have more memories than dreams, life is over." That's true for churches as well. When a church has greater memories than dreams, it will never make a difference in today's world.

To be effective, we must refuse to rely on the past as our source of zeal. A passionate and clear vision for future ministry is the most powerful fuel.

Philadelphia: Ever-Enlarging Willingness to Accept Whatever Challenges God Brings

Christ's final words of approval go to the church in Philadelphia.

> "And to the angel of the church in Philadelphia write:
> He who is holy, who is true, who has the key of David, who opens and no one will shut, and who shuts and no one opens, says this: 'I know your deeds. Behold, I have put before you an open door which no one can shut, because you have a little power, and have kept My word, and have not denied My name.'" (3:7–8)

Jingling the keys of opportunity, Jesus opened a door of hope for this church. The believers may have had only "a little power," but that was OK. They had kept His Word and remained devoted to Him, and Jesus was honoring their faith. Shining in their hearts was this quality: *an ever-enlarging willingness to accept whatever challenges God brings.*

What are the open doors that Christ is setting before our churches today?

- Missionary outreach into previously closed countries

- Contemporary approaches to evangelism

- A broader variety of worship styles

- Renewed calls to prayer

- Mixing of races and cultures

- New strategies in Christian education

- Improved small group ministries

It doesn't matter if we have just "a little power." To pass through these doors, all we need is to keep His Word, remain faithful to His name, and be willing to take up the challenge. These are the keys to becoming a church that makes a difference.

Warnings from Two Churches That Failed to Make a Difference

The five churches mentioned previously multiplied the talents God gave them. Now let's turn to the two churches that buried their talents in the ground. First, the church in Sardis.

> "To the angel of the church in Sardis write:
> He who has the seven Spirits of God and the seven stars, says this: 'I know your deeds, that you have a name that you are alive, but you are dead.'"
> (v. 1)

This church had a good name. People spoke of the assembly in Sardis as an alive congregation. But Jesus, who "searches the minds and hearts" (2:23), pronounced them dead inside. Sadly, this hypocritical church was *guarding its public image but denying the reality of its emptiness.* The warning was this: Don't become more concerned about your image than about the reality of what's happening in your spirit.

The believers in Laodicea had a similar problem. With thumbs in their suspenders, they were crowing, "I am rich, and have become wealthy, and have need of nothing" (3:17a). But Jesus peered into their hearts and announced:

> "'I know your deeds, that you are neither cold nor hot; I wish that you were cold or hot. So because you are lukewarm, and neither hot nor cold, I will spit you out of My mouth.'" (vv. 15–16)

These Christians had *a private opinion of themselves that was completely unrelated to the true facts.* According to Jesus, the truth was they were "wretched and miserable and poor and blind and naked" (v. 17b).

To make a difference in our world, we must be wary of false pride and hypocrisy. People want to see the real us, not the fancy facade we display on Sunday mornings. It's amazing how effective we can be through authenticity. But being authentic requires that we open ourselves before the Lord, that we invite Christ to search our minds and hearts and purge our motives. Then, no matter how tattered our cover may appear, the pages of our lives will tell a story that people will want to read.

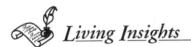 *Living Insights*

Have you ever been duped by a misleading advertisement? At the department store, the package flashed with pizzazz. Glamorous models on the front of the box displayed the product and invited you to join the fun. The package enticed you with its lures: "Sensational!" "It really works!" "Bonus inside!" So you bought it.

But when you unwrapped your prize, disappointment immediately jabbed you in the stomach. The product wasn't flashy at all. It was plastic. The paint was chipped. You felt like throwing it away.

Sometimes our lives can be just as misleading as that advertising. We can display a religious public image that makes glittery but false promises. Others may even buy into our way of living, only to be disappointed when they discover the "real" us.

If you've been showing a flashy false image, take a moment to unwrap the packaging of your life before the Lord. He can already see that your heart is broken. Let Him begin to bring meaning to your emptiness and authenticity to your Christian walk. In the following space, express to Him your innermost thoughts.

_____

_____

_____

_____

_____

It's OK to let others see your struggles. People like truth in advertising, particularly in spiritual matters. Don't be afraid to let others get to know the real you!

Small Group Insights

1. How does your church make a difference? Your small group?

   _____

   _____

2. What facades do we often put up within the evangelical community? Why?

   _____

   _____

3. If Jesus were addressing your church as He did those in Revelation 2–3, how would He characterize it?

   _____

   _____

4. What insights can your church and small group glean from Jesus' words to these churches?

   _____

   _____

Chapter 4

MINISTRY: MOVEMENT OR MONUMENT?

2 Chronicles 26

Centuries ago, Isaiah painted a grand mural of God's glorious coming to earth. The scene is the wilderness, rugged and formidable. In the distance, a voice cries out, "Clear the way! . . .

> Make smooth in the desert a highway for our God.
> Let every valley be lifted up,
> And every mountain and hill be made low;
> And let the rough ground become a plain,
> And the rugged terrain a broad valley;
> Then the *glory* of the Lord will be revealed,
> And all flesh will see it together;
> For the mouth of the Lord has spoken."
> (Isa. 40:3b–5, emphasis added)

The word picture of God's glory—His *kabod*—is vivid in Hebrew. In some contexts, this word means "to be heavy, weighty."[1] God is heavy with splendor and magnificence.

In contrast to God's glory, man's greatness is as insubstantial as a blade of grass that withers "when the breath of the Lord blows upon it" (v. 7). Yet how we loathe to admit that; how tempting it is to claim the credit ourselves for the mighty works He does in and around us. Like a teenager flaunting her mother's diamonds, we sometimes slip His royal robes over our tattered rags and strut around as though they were ours.

Perhaps no one feels that temptation more than those who serve God in a public ministry—those who have been called to hold His glory in sacred trust. Whether their work becomes a movement of God or calcifies into a monument to themselves depends on one crucial factor: who gets the glory.

---

1. R. Laird Harris, Gleason L. Archer, Jr., and Bruce K. Waltke, eds., *Theological Wordbook of the Old Testament* (Chicago, Ill.: Moody Press, 1980), vol. 1, p. 426.

A Formula to Follow

Let's return to Isaiah to discover an important formula for those who desire to build movements, not monuments. In chapter 42, the Lord made several promises to His number one Servant, the Messiah:

> "I am the Lord, I have called you in righteousness,
> I will also hold you by the hand and watch over you,
> And I will appoint you as a covenant to the people,
> As a light to the nations,
> To open blind eyes,
> To bring out prisoners from the dungeon
> And those who dwell in darkness from the prison."
> (42:6–7)

The Lord not only called Christ, He promised to guide Him—"I will also hold you by the hand"; protect Him—"watch over you"; and use Him as "a light to the nations." As fellow servants with Christ, we carry on His ministry. We, too, are called, guided, protected, and used as lights to open eyes blinded by sin. But we must always keep in mind the Lord's next words:

> "I am the Lord, that is My name;
> I will not give My glory to another,
> Nor My praise to graven images." (v. 8)

Having declared His name in verse 6, the Lord repeats it here for emphasis: "I am the Lord!" Fleeting humanity will build its idols and empires, but God will never abdicate His divine position to them. Glory and praise are God's alone.

The elements of verse 8 contain a formula for keeping our ministries moving forward.

- First, *remember His name.*

- Second, *reflect His character.*

- Third, *rejoice in His praises.*

No matter how gifted we are, no matter how valuable, no matter how many people hang on our words or listen to our songs or heed our counsel—we have no right to take God's name lightly, eclipse His glory, or steal His praise. As soon as we do, the movement of God halts and a monument to our glory is erected; and how quickly those monuments come crashing down, taking us with them. A tragic example of this rise and fall is found in the story of King Uzziah.

An Example to Learn From

Uzziah made his entrance onto the pages of Scripture with great fanfare. He was the new king, the son of Amaziah, who had just been assassinated after turning away from the Lord. The royal robes, along with the hopes of the nation, had been placed on his shoulders—a heavy responsibility for a boy of only sixteen years (2 Chron. 26:1–3).

In his early days, Uzziah bore the weight well. Like his father before his rebellion,

> he did right in the sight of the Lord according to all that his father Amaziah had done. He continued to seek God in the days of Zechariah, who had understanding through the vision of God; and as long as he sought the Lord, God prospered him. (26:4–5)

As the years passed, his smooth teenager's face changed into the bearded face of manhood and then the gray head of middle age, but his heart remained the same. He was committed to doing things the right way, God's way. Because of his faith, God allowed him to prosper for fifty-two years—as a captain of the military, as a builder, and as a farmer. Look at some of the accomplishments the chronicler pinned to the king's chest like medals:

- Conquering the Philistines and Judah's other enemies (vv. 6–8)

- Constructing fortifications in Jerusalem and the wilderness area (vv. 9–10a)

- Hewing cisterns, raising livestock, and developing the land for crops (v. 10b)

- Building a vast, well-equipped, and highly trained army (vv. 11–15a)

With God's help, Uzziah had become a mighty king. Slowly and secretly, though, pride had been slinking into his heart, and he had begun to polish his medals more than praise the Lord.

> Hence his fame spread afar, for he was marvelously helped *until* he was strong. (v. 15b, emphasis added)

The fate of Uzziah's entire life hinged on that one word *until*.

31

For, as the chronicler sadly records,

> But when he became strong, his heart was so proud
> that he acted corruptly . . . (v. 16a)

With his achievements bannered over Jerusalem and the people's accolades ringing in his ears, Uzziah believed his own press. And that's when his demise began—when his favorite piece of palace furniture became the mirror. He borrowed the Lord's name. He absorbed His glory. He took the praises that should have gone to God. No longer did he see how the Lord helped him get where he was. Once a movement of God, Uzziah's kingdom was now a monument to himself, and the Lord was about to remove its foundation of blessing.

Signs of a Monument in the Making

From the precarious peak of Uzziah's pride, let's identify a few warning signs of a monument in the making.

When Greater Battles Are Fought Within than Without

The first stone slips into place when greater battles are fought within than without. When Uzziah was fighting the Philistines, he was focused on the Lord. But when he started to fight for his own image, the battleground moved from the field to his heart. When any ministry leader no longer battles "Philistines" but becomes more and more preoccupied with himself or herself, a monument is starting to take shape.

When More Attention Is Directed to the Leader than to the Lord

If people mention the leader's name more than the Lord's, if they measure their lives by his or her standards of holiness rather than Scripture's, if they cater to his or her whims without questioning them, then the ministry is a monument to the leader and has begun slipping away from God's favor.

Tragically, most prideful leaders don't even realize what's happening. They're so accustomed to people giving them attention that they don't smell the stink of arrogance rising from their me-first attitude. Egotism desensitizes them to their own foolishness. The chronicler says Uzziah "was so proud that he acted corruptly" (v. 16a). Of course, Uzziah didn't see it that way. Pride had beguiled him, beckoning from alluring, dangerous heights.

When God's Help Is Nice but Not Essential

The third sign of a monument in the making is the leader's attitude that God's help is nice but not essential. After preaching a hundred sermons, it's easy to coast through number 101; when the songs have become old and familiar, it's easy to go through the motions one more time. Some leaders get so used to speaking for God that the Lord's glory loses its weight. They start throwing their own weight around. A foolish bravado enters their souls: "I've done this before. I can do it again. I can do anything."

Inflated with his own self-importance, Uzziah thought he could enter into the holy presence of God Himself:

> . . . he was unfaithful to the Lord his God, for he entered the temple of the Lord to burn incense on the altar of incense. Then Azariah the priest entered after him and with him eighty priests of the Lord, valiant men. They opposed Uzziah the king and said to him, "It is not for you, Uzziah, to burn incense to the Lord, but for the priests, the sons of Aaron who are consecrated to burn incense. Get out of the sanctuary, for you have been unfaithful and will have no honor from the Lord God." (vv. 16b–18)

The Hebrew word translated *honor* here is also the word *kabod*. The king longed for the Lord's glory, but it was God's alone. It was dangerous to even come near it. Seeing Uzziah walking toward the fire of God's glory, the priests rushed to pull him back.

When Worthwhile Reproofs Are Resisted Rather than Received

Uzziah's response to their protests illustrates the fourth sign of monument construction.

> But Uzziah, with a censer in his hand for burning incense, was enraged[2] . . . (v. 19a)

Out of Uzziah's proud heart flowed a sea of raging indignation that crashed upon the priests. How dare they oppose the king!

---

2. The Hebrew word for *enraged*, *zaaph*, is the verb form of the noun used in Jonah 1:15 to describe the raging sea that engulfed the disobedient prophet.

According to Proverbs, "He who reproves a wicked man gets insults for himself" (Prov. 9:7b). Uzziah's anger pointed to the wickedness brewing inside him. If we truly desire to live God's way, we'll welcome correction with grace and humility. Had Uzziah done that, he would have spared himself the immense pain that followed.

When the Consequences of Sin Are Ignored

Tragically, Uzziah wasn't even concerned about the consequences of his sin . . . until they hit him in the face.

> . . . while he was enraged with the priests, the leprosy broke out on his forehead before the priests in the house of the Lord, beside the altar of incense. Azariah the chief priest and all the priests looked at him, and behold, he was leprous on his forehead; and they hurried him out of there, and he himself also hastened to get out because the Lord had smitten him. (2 Chron. 26:19b–20)

Uzziah ended his magnificent reign cut off from the temple and the nation, quarantined as a leper in a separate house (v. 21). And when he finally died, how did the people remember him—as a military hero? a visionary builder? a cultivator of the land? Read on to find out.

> So Uzziah slept with his fathers, and they buried him with his fathers in the field of the grave which belonged to the kings, for they said, "He is a leper." (v. 23a)

Grasping for glory, Uzziah died in infamy. His story flashes a warning sign: Take seriously the consequences of sin. In arrogance, we tend to blame others for the backlash of our wrongdoing. We feel sorry for ourselves. We call it "bad luck" and regret getting caught. However, as the New Testament writer James reminds us, we have no one to blame but ourselves:

> But each one is tempted when he is carried away and enticed by his own lust. Then when lust has conceived, it gives birth to sin; and when sin is accomplished, it brings forth death. (James 1:14–15)

Conclusion

Ministry monuments result in disaster. Movements of God, however, accomplish amazing things. Sixteen-year-old Uzziah never imagined the wealth and power his little nation would produce. You may be a minister, a church leader, a Sunday school teacher, or a counselor. You may head up a committee or lead a small Bible study. God can do remarkable things through you as you depend upon His help. Always remember, though, who gets the glory!

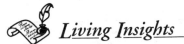 *Living Insights*

A monument is anything we build to impress people with our greatness. We can erect monuments to ourselves anywhere—in our homes, at work, or at church. Our houses can become monoliths to our material success. Our children can even become monuments to our parenting skills. Our status on the job or in the community can be a pillar to our leadership power. The growth of a church can be a monument to our religious zeal.

As you examine your life, have you built any monuments to yourself? Where are they?

_____

_____

_____

_____

Pulling down these towers of pride involves changing our perspective toward our accomplishments. It is God who "gives to all people life and breath and all things" (Acts 17:25). All our successes spring from His well of grace.

Try applying Isaiah's formula for giving God the glory concerning one of the "monuments" you listed. First, *remember His name.* Sign His name to your accomplishment as the One who gets the ultimate credit. Second, *reflect His character.* Think of some ways your skills—leadership, parenting, singing, and so on—can mirror His qualities, such as patience, love, or compassion. Third, *rejoice in His praises.* Express your thanks to Him for the victories He wins for you.

Small Group Insights

1. Offer some examples of biblical characters who gave God glory. How were they blessed?

   _____

   _____

   _____

   _____

2. Name a person who failed to glorify God and who took credit for himself or herself. What were the circumstances? What happened as a result?

   _____

   _____

   _____

   _____

3. How can you serve the others in your church, family, small group, and community with humility?

   _____

   _____

   _____

   _____

4. What steps can you take this week to demolish any monuments you may have constructed in your life? How can you experience God's movement in new ways?

   _____

   _____

   _____

   _____

Chapter 5

THINKING RIGHT ABOUT THE CHURCH

Survey of 1 Timothy

D id you know that the church has a fragrance? The apostle Paul called it a "sweet aroma":

> But thanks be to God, who always leads us in triumph in Christ, and manifests through us the sweet aroma of the knowledge of Him in every place. For we are a fragrance of Christ to God among those who are being saved and among those who are perishing. (2 Cor. 2:14–15)

In the past few years, unfortunately, the stench of sin has invaded some high-profile ministries, obscuring the fragrance of Christ. Catching wind of these moral failings, the media have focused the world's attention on them, exploiting every sordid detail. Smelling only the rankness, the world has decided that *all* the church is that way. But the world's thinking is wrong; there's still a lot about the church that is fragrant.

Even so, our reputation has been dealt a staggering blow. The body of Christ has become a punching bag for people eager to poke fun. City governments, school boards, and courts seem to have lost their trust in the church as a positive influence. Even Christians are having their doubts.

It's time to push aside the negative thinking and draw our attention to God's perspective of His church. He smells the sin, but He also breathes in the sweet aroma. In his first letter to Timothy, Paul highlights six fragrant qualities that will help us think rightly about the church.

We Are a Body That Is Healthy and Balanced

Emanating from the first chapter of Paul's letter are the qualities of health and balance in the church. These characteristics are particularly appealing because we live in a world careening out of control, a world of grotesque extremes.

One side of town revels in its private tennis courts, five-car garages, and multi-million-dollar homes, while on the other side of the tracks ragged people push their belongings in grocery carts and huddle in doorways for shelter. The pleasures of sex are pursued to excess while relentless suffering overflows AIDS wards. Movies, television, and music swing from the sublime and spellbinding to the violent and obscene—the industry doesn't entertain so much as infect.

To a world teetering on the brink, the church offers moral health and spiritual balance. Paul exhorted Timothy to make his church a secure place for frazzled people searching for truth.

> . . . instruct certain men not to teach strange doctrines, nor to pay attention to myths and endless genealogies, which give rise to mere speculation rather than furthering the administration of God which is by faith. (1 Tim. 1:3b–4)

God has placed His people here for the purpose of instructing each other and counteracting the world's "speculations." Only the church offers these three counterpoints to the messages of a lost society:

- *The goal of our instruction—love:* "But the goal of our instruction is love from a pure heart and a good conscience and a sincere faith" (v. 5).

- *The core of our message—the Gospel:* "It is a trustworthy statement, deserving full acceptance, that Christ Jesus came into the world to save sinners, among whom I am foremost of all" (v. 15).

- *The object of our worship—the King eternal:* "Now to the King eternal, immortal, invisible, the only God, be honor and glory forever and ever. Amen" (v. 17).

You won't hear about pure love, the salvation message, and Christ the King in a secular classroom. High society won't be all abuzz about them. The government won't offer them to you. Hollywood won't flash them on a movie screen. Nor will your workplace provide them as benefits. Only the church can lead you to Christ and His redeeming way of life.

We Are People Committed to Prayer

We pride ourselves in our high-tech ability to meet our own needs. Need money right away? No problem. Slide the card and out comes the cash. Need a quick meal? No problem. Pop the package in the microwave and out comes dinner. However, concerning the deeper needs of the heart, technology turns us cold. Reaching beyond our surface needs, the church ushers us into God's presence and, through prayer, plugs us into His power. Notice the emphasis Paul places on prayer in chapter 2:

> First of all, then, I urge that entreaties and prayers, petitions and thanksgivings, be made on behalf of all men, for kings and all who are in authority, so that we may lead a tranquil and quiet life in all godliness and dignity. This is good and acceptable in the sight of God our Savior, who desires all men to be saved and to come to the knowledge of the truth. . . .
> Therefore I want the men in every place to pray, lifting up holy hands, without wrath and dissension. (vv. 1–4, 8)

Prayer is not passive contemplation. It's an active statement of confidence in God's authority over us. It's an invitation for Him to explore our secret passages—our fears, our longings, our pain. It gives Him permission to do whatever He wishes in our lives, whenever He pleases, for only God knows what is best for us. Prayer may not change our circumstances, but it always changes *us*. It builds our faith and develops in us a deep-seated sense of contentment. The world has nothing to compare with the peace that comes through prayer.

We Are a Representation of God's Unchanging Standards

In chapter 3, Paul lists the qualifications for leaders in the church. These standards haven't changed since Paul penned them almost two thousand years ago. Nowhere in the world is there a job description like this one. Take a look at the level of excellence the church's leadership represents:

> An overseer, then, must be above reproach, the husband of one wife, temperate, prudent, respectable, hospitable, able to teach, not addicted to wine or pugnacious, but gentle, peaceable, free from the love of money. He must be one who manages his own household well, keeping his children under control

with all dignity (but if a man does not know how to manage his own household, how will he take care of the church of God?), and not a new convert, so that he will not become conceited and fall into the condemnation incurred by the devil. And he must have a good reputation with those outside the church, so that he will not fall into reproach and the snare of the devil. (vv. 2–7)

For the most part, the same list of qualifications applies to deacons and deaconesses, whose job descriptions appear in verses 8–13.[1] In verse 15, Paul refers to the whole body of believers as "the household of God," "the church of the living God," and "the pillar and support of the truth." The Lord calls *all* of us, not just the leaders, to a higher standard—as Paul writes, "so that you will know how one ought to conduct himself."

However, a list of qualifications is not the final measure of our conduct. Jesus Himself is the ultimate standard:

> He who was revealed in the flesh,
> Was vindicated in the Spirit,
> Seen by angels,
> Proclaimed among the nations,
> Believed on in the world,
> Taken up in glory. (v. 16b)

And He *never* changes.

We Are a Force for Good in Bad Times

According to chapter 4, bad times will come—indeed, they are here now. Do you recognize in our world the characteristics Paul warns us to watch for?

- Defection (v. 1a)

- Deception (v. 1b)

- Demonism (v. 1c)

- Hypocrisy (v. 2)

- Legalism and asceticism (v. 3a)

---

1. The "women" referred to in verse 11 could be the deacons' wives or female leaders, sometimes called deaconesses.

But in the midst of this whirlwind of evil, the church stands as a bastion of righteousness—as long as its members act out the roles Paul describes to Timothy.

- Good servants, nourished on faith and sound doctrine (v. 6b)
- Disciplined disciples, whose goal is godliness (v. 7b)
- Exemplary teachers, sharing the hope of Christ (vv. 10–11)

In verses 14–16, Paul tutors us along with Timothy in how to live up to our high callings. To be a *good servant*, he says, "do not neglect the spiritual gift within you" (v. 14a).[2] To be a *disciplined disciple*, he admonishes, we should "take pains with these things," meaning we need to cultivate our spiritual gifts and a Christlike character. "Be absorbed in them, so that your progress will be evident to all" (v. 15). To be an *exemplary teacher*, he encourages us to "pay close attention to yourself and to your teaching; persevere in these things, for as you do this you will ensure salvation both for yourself and for those who hear you" (v. 16).

Being a force for good doesn't just happen. We must exercise our spiritual gifts, take pains to live godly lives in an ungodly world, and measure ourselves closely against Christ and His teaching.

What about you? How well are you doing concerning these things?

We Are a Model of Compassion with Discernment

In 1 Timothy 5, Paul addresses the issue of the church's support of widows. Pension plans and Social Security programs didn't exist in the first century, so church members pooled their money to help widows in need, expressing the compassionate side of Christianity. However, there was another side of the church that steadied the ship—discernment.

How best to help the homeless, the drug abusers, and the poor is often difficult to determine—we want to be generous with our money and acceptance, but these must be given within limits. For example, rather than cash, some people need confrontation about their wrong choices. The church is one of the few places where moral definitions and the truth about responsibilities are taught.

2. Paul lists the spiritual gifts in Romans 12:3–8; 1 Corinthians 12:4–11, 28–31; and Ephesians 4:11–13. For more information about spiritual gifts, see the study guide *He Gave Gifts*, written by Bryce Klabunde, from the Bible-teaching ministry of Charles R. Swindoll (Anaheim, Calif.: Insight for Living, 1992).

Paul gives Timothy discerning counsel about widows in verses 3–16; encourages the church to pay a fair salary to those in the ministry (vv. 17–18); and shows the proper way to confront a church leader of wrongdoing (vv. 19–20). He also points the way on issues concerning ordaining ministers, using wine, and evaluating a person's true character (vv. 21–25). These gray areas with no pat answers are hammered out in the church, where God's will is sought and determined.

The Church Is a Source of Reliable Information

In the sixth chapter, the church assumes its role as an amplifier of truth. With megaphone in hand, Paul preaches on at least seven subjects in this section:

1. One's occupation (vv. 1–2)

2. Doctrinal truths (v. 3)

3. Relational conflicts (vv. 4–5)

4. Personal contentment (vv. 6–8)

5. Money (vv. 9–11, 17–19)

6. Priorities (v. 12)

7. Life and lifestyle (vv. 13–16, 20–21)

The world may resist the truth of God's Word, but the church isn't in the business of tickling people's ears. Our job is to wrestle with the precepts of Scripture and tell ourselves and others what we need to hear—which may be painful at times. But we can be sure that when we do our job well, when we stick with Scripture, the information we dispense is reliable. We can bank our lives on it.

Conclusion

Our world may turn up its nose at the church. It may think that all churches fit the money-grubbing, hypocritical stereotype. But the truth is, there are many more fragrant churches than rotten ones. There is far more good than wrong. There are far more leaders with pure motives than ones with selfish motives. The sweet aroma of Christ is everywhere in the church. Let's take the time to enjoy it.

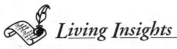 *Living Insights*

Through the flowers, a few weeds always find room to poke their noxious heads. Have you noticed any weedlike sins cropping up in your life? Maybe you see an unhealthy or out-of-balance attitude sprouting. Perhaps a resistance to prayer. Or a reluctance to reflect God's standard. Possibly you're neglecting God's call to be a force for good, to show compassion, or to be a resource of scriptural information. If so, rather than hurriedly snipping those weeds with a quick prayer, choose one to dig out and remove it from the roots. Which weed would you like to target?

_____

_____

The roots may be deeper than you think. Do you need help pulling them out? If so, who could you ask to give you a hand in this area?

_____

_____

What's your plan to get rid of this unwelcome plant in your flower bed? Try to be specific.

_____

_____

_____

Got your tools and gloves? OK. Let's do some gardening!

Small Group Insights

1. How does your church impact the world? What are its vital ministries?

_____

_____

_____

_____

_____

_____

2. How does the world influence your church? Give specific examples.

_____

_____

_____

_____

_____

_____

3. How can your small group be a force for good in dark times?

_____

_____

_____

_____

4. What steps can you take to make your "aroma of Christ" more fragrant?

_____

_____

_____

_____

_____

Chapter 6

FLEXING WITH
A FUTURE IN FLUX
Acts 11:1–18

The church has always been known for its resolute spirit. Built upon the solid bedrock of Jesus Christ and reinforced by the granite pillars of the prophets and apostles, the church stands on the plain of history as a fortress of truth. Philosophies and religions rise and fall, but the church and the Gospel it defends remain forever.

Problems occur, though, when we think that because the church's *message* is changeless, the church's *methods* must be changeless too. *How* we worship becomes as important as *who* we worship. Eventually, we end up guarding our fifty-year-old approaches to ministry with the same tenacity we use in defending the Scriptures. Viewing new ideas with a suspicious eye, we entrench ourselves in traditional routines and hunker down behind the concrete walls of our closed minds.

While the church stands still, however, the world moves on. How can we expect to make a difference in a rapidly changing world if we're living in the past? Are we ready for the changes the future will bring?

Questions That Deserve an Answer

Are *you* ready for the future? The technological advances of the new millennium promise to be earth shattering. Some predict that by the year 2010, biomonitoring devices the size of wristwatches will provide wearers with up-to-the-minute data about their health status. Tiny electronic microchips implanted in a person's forearm will transmit messages to a computer that controls the heating and lighting systems of "smart" buildings. And as technology goes global and electronic communication reaches lightning speed, ninety percent of the world's approximately 6,000 languages could become extinct by 2100.[1]

Portions of this chapter have been adapted from "Getting Out of God's Way," from the study guide *The Growth of an Expanding Mission*, written by Bryce Klabunde, from the Bible-teaching ministry of Charles R. Swindoll (Anaheim, Calif.: Insight for Living, 1992).

1. CNN.com, at http://www.cnn.com/2000/US/01/01predictions, accessed on July 9, 2002.

So much change makes us dizzy. And it makes us wonder, Where is God in all this?

Where in Heaven Is God in All This?

Is He sitting in heaven, stooped over and wringing His hands—too old to comprehend our newfangled technology and too out of touch to understand our problems? Definitely not. "If there is a God at all," wrote J. B. Phillips,

> he must be "big enough" to fit into the modern scene (and that naturally means a conception of the Creator a million times greater than that held even a century ago).[2]

With each new universe of knowledge we unlock, God is there, waiting for us to come in and explore His creation. He's not worried about the future. In fact, God looks forward to it and the changes He's going to bring about. He told Isaiah:

> "Do not call to mind the former things,
> Or ponder things of the past.
> Behold, I will do something new,
> Now it will spring forth . . ."
> "I proclaim to you new things from this time,
> Even hidden things which you have not known.
> They are created now and not long ago;
> And before today you have not heard them,
> So that you will not say, 'Behold, I knew them.'"
> (Isa. 43:18–19a; 48:6b–7)

God is creating all the time. He's a God of new ideas, of innovation, of change.

Who in the Church Is Ready for the Challenge?

Church analyst Lawrence Richards says that, when faced with the possibility of change, most people reflect one of three personality types.

- *Innovators:* These people embrace change enthusiastically and are willing to try any new idea that offers the hope of progress.

2. J. B. Phillips, *God Our Contemporary* (New York, N.Y.: Macmillan Co., 1960), p. 3.

- *Conservatives:* These people are what we might call "maintainers." They are cautious about change and want to have all the facts firmly in place before launching a new plan.

- *Inhibitors:* These people resist change, regardless of the facts and no matter how feasible the plan may be.

Richards' findings further reveal that ten percent of the people in an organization are innovators, eighty percent are conservatives or maintainers, and ten percent are inhibitors.[3] From these statistics, we can see that most people, though cautious, are willing to follow a new course if they are convinced it is the right way. Are you like that? If so, you're in good company.

Issues Then and Now

The apostle Peter was a classic maintainer. Born a Jew, he was steeped in the traditions of his forefathers. And, although Jesus had drawn him out of the seas of legalism and onto the shores of grace, he was still a Jew, dragging with him a long list of dos and don'ts. One of the blackest sins on the Jewish list was fraternizing with Gentiles—entering their homes, eating their food, attending their gatherings. As the Gospel rippled out of Jerusalem into surrounding Gentile regions, this wall between the groups presented the early church with its first major obstacle. But for Peter, the wall was about to come tumbling down in a most dramatic way.

While praying one day, Peter saw a fantastic vision of a great sheet full of all kinds of animals being lowered from the sky. Then he heard a voice from heaven: "Get up, Peter, kill and eat!" (Acts 10:13). Of course, conservative Peter hesitated.

"By no means, Lord, for I have never eaten anything unholy and unclean." (v. 14)

But the Lord replied,

"What God has cleansed, no longer consider unholy." (v. 15)

Three times the vision appeared to Peter, and three times he resisted the Lord's revolutionary command. Then some men, sent by a God-fearing Gentile named Cornelius, rapped on the door and

3. Lawrence O. Richards, *A New Face for the Church* (Grand Rapids, Mich.: Zondervan Publishing House, 1970), p. 43.

asked for Peter to come with them to Caesarea—Gentile country. As Peter accompanied them to Cornelius' house, the vision began to make sense. "God has shown me," he said upon arrival, "that I should not call any man unholy or unclean" (v. 28b). With delight, he explained the Gospel to the people gathered there, and they believed in Christ. To the amazement of the Jews who had come with Peter, God immediately poured out His Holy Spirit on them, and they began speaking in tongues just like the Jews in Jerusalem at Pentecost (see vv. 44–46).

This encounter released the chains of legalism that still hung on Peter from his Jewish past. Now everything was clean in Christ— even Gentiles. Imagine him sitting down for dinner with his new Gentile friends, staring at a plateful of pork. "In Christ, I'm free to eat this," he reassures himself, gulping down the surprisingly delicious nonkosher meal. God was bringing change into Peter's life, and frankly, he was enjoying it!

Institutionalism

The time soon came for Peter to return home to Jerusalem. But before he arrived, the news of his association with Cornelius had already made the rounds.

> Now the apostles and the brethren who were throughout Judea heard that the Gentiles also had received the word of God. And when Peter came up to Jerusalem, those who were circumcised took issue with him, saying, "You went to uncircumcised men and ate with them." (11:1–3)

Peter no sooner stepped foot in the city before the Jewish Christians there began pointing fingers and wagging tongues. "Shame on you, Peter!" "How could you, Peter!" "You've gone liberal, Peter!"

Institutional Judaism was rotting the church from the inside. Make no mistake; Peter's accusers were believers. They were on his side. However, unlike them, Peter was willing to flex with God's creative plan.

Before we write these people off as inhibitors, though, let's continue the story as Peter explained to them the facts of the case.

Transformation

He knew that the Jerusalem believers needed to be transformed just as he had been. So, "in orderly sequence," he calmly led them across the same bridge of change on which he had journeyed, from the vision to the visit with Cornelius (see vv. 4–14). He saved the best part of the story for last:

> "And as I began to speak, the Holy Spirit fell upon them just as He did upon us at the beginning. And I remembered the word of the Lord, how He used to say, 'John baptized with water, but you will be baptized with the Holy Spirit.'" (vv. 15–16)

Fixation

Then he reached the pinnacle of his presentation:

> "Therefore if God gave to them the same gift as He gave to us also after believing in the Lord Jesus Christ, who was I that I could stand in God's way?" (v. 17)

Peter had walked the people over to the shore of something completely new. Now they had to decide whether to step off with him or turn their backs on God's way. If they refused the truth, they would have had what we might call a fixation—what *Merriam-Webster's* defines as "an obsessive or unhealthy . . . attachment."[4]

When confronted with change, we tend to fixate on the securities of the status quo. We cling to the rail of the bridge, fearful of anything new. People with fixations block what God is trying to do. They are inhibitors—busy, perhaps, in the Lord's work, but rigid toward fresh ideas. Peter had asked himself, "Who was I that I could stand in God's way?" And now he asked the people the same question by implication: "Who are *you* to stand in God's way?" Would they loosen their grip on the past and accept God's new plan for the Gentiles?

Alteration

Luke records their response:

> When they heard this, they quieted down and glorified God, saying, "Well then, God has granted to the Gentiles also the repentance that leads to life." (v. 18)

---

4. *Merriam-Webster's Collegiate Dictionary*, 10th ed., see "fixation."

To their credit, each one of them stepped off the bridge and followed Peter into the future. Once there, they gloried in God's marvelous grace—the grace that was bigger than any one of them could have imagined.

Answers That Are Right, but Uncomfortable

When faced with change, how should we respond? Five answers emerge from Peter's story.

It is essential that we remain calm. When Peter finished presenting his case for change, the people "quieted down" (v. 18). As we consider the new ways God might lead us, let's do so with a quiet, patient spirit.

It is essential that we glorify God. After the believers quieted down and accepted what Peter had said, they "glorified God" (v. 18). Any vision for the future must be for God's glory. We're not in the business of building little empires for ourselves but of building God's kingdom.

It is essential that we walk through doors God opens. Like doors in a hallway, many exciting opportunities await us in the future. And when they open up, we need to push aside our instinct to hang back. Instead, we must step forward with confidence and faith.

It is essential that we willingly flex and adapt. Willingly is the key word. Don't let *no* always be the first word out of your mouth. If you tend to be an inhibitor, practice saying yes a few times and try being open to new ideas.

It is essential that we continually evaluate. What's happening in the world? Is our ministry still meeting people's needs? Should we toss out a certain program that isn't working anymore? What new door is God cracking open? These kinds of questions keep us flexible and ready to face whatever future God has in store for us.

 Living Insights

Imagine yourself in the following situations. How would you respond? "Sure, let's do it!"? "Well, maybe."? Or "Absolutely not!"? In the blank after each statement, write down your response.

1. Your friend suggests trying a new restaurant that features international food you've never eaten before. _____

2. One week before your family vacation, your spouse suggests a change of plan. _____

3. Your son asks if he can save his money so he can buy a pet snake. _____

4. Your pastor suggests that the church start a cross-cultural ministry to minorities in the neighborhood. _____

5. The music minister proposes using a variety of instruments besides just the piano and organ during the worship time at church. _____

6. The youth minister would like to use the sanctuary for Christian outreach concerts for local high school students. _____

By your reactions to these situations and, perhaps, other situations in which you face change, can you determine whether you are mostly an innovator, a conservative/maintainer, or an inhibitor? Give a brief illustration from your life that verifies your evaluation of yourself.

_____

_____

_____

When presented with change, it's helpful to first recognize your personality type and understand your natural reactions. Then you can follow the five steps we outlined in the chapter:

Remain calm.

Determine whether this change will glorify God.

Go through the doors God opens.

Be willing to flex and adapt.

Continually evaluate present programs for ways to change and grow.

Are you facing a change in your life? In the following space, work through your feelings about this change using the five steps.

_____

_____

_____

_____

_____

Small Group Insights

1. Think about the dynamics of your church, small group, and family. Who are the innovators? The conservatives? The inhibitors?

   _____

   _____

   _____

2. How are each of these roles important in the body of Christ?

   _____

   _____

   _____

3. How would you characterize yourself according to these categories?

   _____

   _____

   _____

4. How do you think you and your group will need to adjust to the changing environment in your church, small group, school, and workplace in the future?

   _____

   _____

   _____

Chapter 7

HOW TO HELP
OUR NATION SURVIVE

2 Chronicles 7:11–22

The year was 1961. As a January wind chilled the air, John F. Kennedy accepted the office of president of the United States and fired up our patriotic spirit with these immortal words:

> "And so, my fellow Americans, ask not what your country can do for you; ask what you can do for your country."[1]

What *can* we do for our country? We can pay taxes, vote, obey the laws, defend the nation against invaders. These are worthwhile contributions, but there must be something more—something deeper.

Today, our nation is fighting for its survival. Threatening us, however, are not the "usual" social diseases that torment underdeveloped countries—poor sanitation, poverty, starvation. Ours is a struggle of the soul, with cancerous sin spreading insidiously through our nation's vital organs. Every day, another family collapses from compromised morality, another business dies from lack of ethics, another young person falls from weakened values.

What can we do for our country? How can we help our nation survive? These questions are too personal to be relegated to a president to answer. We must turn to our Maker for His wise counsel.

A Day of Dedication

Almost three thousand years before John F. Kennedy celebrated his ascent to power, another young leader was reveling in his landmark achievement. Solomon, the son of King David, had just completed the temple that his father had only dreamed about. After years of work, Solomon's expert craftsmen had tapped the last stone in place and hung the last golden door. A beehive of workers had polished the lamps, snuffers, bowls, and fire pans to gleaming perfection. God's permanent house was ready for habitation.

---

1. John F. Kennedy, as quoted in *Bartlett's Familiar Quotations*, 15th ed., rev. and enl., ed. Emily Morison Beck (Boston, Mass.: Little, Brown and Co., 1980), p. 890.

While the king and the people were making sacrifices to welcome God's glory into the new temple, an army of priests carried the ark of the covenant into the Holy of Holies. Solomon then lifted his hands in an ardent prayer, dedicating the temple and the nation to the Lord's service. When he finished,

> fire came down from heaven and consumed the burnt offering and the sacrifices, and the glory of the Lord filled the house. The priests could not enter into the house of the Lord because the glory of the Lord filled the Lord's house. All the sons of Israel, seeing the fire come down and the glory of the Lord upon the house, bowed down on the pavement with their faces to the ground, and they worshiped and gave praise to the Lord, saying, "Truly He is good, truly His lovingkindness is everlasting." (2 Chron. 7:1b–3)

For days the worshiping and sacrificing continued, reaching a peak in a day of "solemn assembly," after which the people joyfully returned home (vv. 4–10). The king's heart must have pounded with pride as he went to bed that night. What an accomplishment! He had "successfully completed all that he had planned on doing in the house of the Lord and in his palace" (v. 11).

Painstakingly, he had designed the temple to meet God's holy requirements. At great expense, he had led his people in a magnificent worship service. This had been the pinnacle event of his life, and now it was over. The crowds had gone, and the noise had died down. The moment was his to savor as he basked in the afterglow and replayed the magnificent music in his mind. Then, without warning, while the king rested in the darkness, a Visitor slipped into the room.

A Night of Visitation

With no one else around, "the Lord appeared to Solomon at night" (v. 12a). It was just God and His man, together in the stillness. During this intimate encounter, the Lord chose three subjects to counsel the king about: the temple, the people, and Solomon himself.

God's House

Filling the room with His divine presence, the Lord first encouraged Solomon with these words:

> "I have heard your prayer and have chosen this place

for Myself as a house of sacrifice." (v. 12b)

Pleasing the Lord had been Solomon's sole intention from the moment he launched the project; how grateful he must have been to receive this affirmation.

God called the temple "a house of sacrifice," perhaps to remind Solomon of its purpose. This was a place of meeting, where contrite souls could find mercy and where God in His holiness could embrace His people. The doors of this house must always be open and the sacrifices, always burning—-sacrifices of animals, of praise, and of prayer. God had claimed this building as *His*. No self-avowed messiah must depose Him. The nation must remain faithful to Him alone, no matter what the future may hold.

God's Nation

In the days ahead, the spirit of celebration would most likely fade, and the people would be tempted to start drifting away from the Lord. If that should happen, God might have to test His nation in the following ways:

> "If I shut up the heavens so that there is no rain, or if I command the locust to devour the land, or if I send pestilence among My people . . ." (v. 13; compare 6:26–31)

Drought, famine, plague. How could the nation survive? As we endure the consequences of our own sin, we ask the same question. God's answer to Solomon blows across culture and time to give us a refreshing wind of hope.

> ". . . [if] My people who are called by My name humble themselves and pray and seek My face and turn from their wicked ways, then I will hear from heaven, will forgive their sin and will heal their land." (7:14)

From this verse we can see that God expects four things from His people:

- The attitude of a servant—"humble themselves"
- A spirit of dependence—"and pray"
- A willingness to wait—"seek My face"
- A response of obedience—"turn from their wicked ways"

55

Israel's past heritage would not be enough to help the people endure God's discipline. They would have to return to Him with humble and dependent hearts, willing to wait for His deliverance. That's not all, though; they must show their change of attitude through their actions. In sailing terms, they must come about—change their heading from pursuing sin to pursuing righteousness.

In return, God promised that their prayers would get His attention—"I will hear from heaven" (v. 14b)—and that He would "forgive their sin" as He witnessed their humble spirit. He also promised to heal the nation as He saw the people changing the direction of their lives. Disobedience to God's law is an internal disease that requires divine healing. All other remedies merely treat the symptoms. And, although God is a righteous Judge who, in His sovereignty, disciplines the people, He is also a loving Physician. Eagerly, He waits for His people to come to Him:

> "Now My eyes will be open and My ears attentive to the prayer offered in this place. For now I have chosen and consecrated this house that My name may be there forever, and My eyes and My heart will be there perpetually." (vv. 15–16)

The temple was not just an inspiring cathedral for choirs and priests, it was a place where people could come to experience God personally. Centuries later, although Solomon's building was gone, Jesus nevertheless respected the temple for its original purpose. Seeing the religious charlatans exploiting the pilgrims who were seeking atonement there, Jesus

> entered the temple and drove out all those who were buying and selling in the temple, and overturned the tables of the money changers and the seats of those who were selling doves. And He said to them, "It is written, 'My house shall be called a house of prayer'; but you are making it a robbers' den."
> And the blind and the lame came to Him in the temple, and He healed them. (Matt. 21:12–14)

Healing, mercy, and prayer—that's what the temple was designed for.

God's Leader

Turning from His temple to His leader, the Lord offered Solomon

56

two futures, each showing how his spiritual walk could potentially influence the nation. In one hand, the Lord extended a gracious promise; in the other, a serious warning. First, the positive side:

> "As for you, if you walk before Me as your father David walked, even to do according to all that I have commanded you, and will keep My statutes and My ordinances, then I will establish your royal throne as I covenanted with your father David, say-ing, 'You shall not lack a man to be ruler in Israel.'" (2 Chron. 7:17–18)

Then God revealed the negative side:

> "But if you turn away and forsake My statutes and My commandments which I have set before you, and go and serve other gods and worship them, then I will uproot you from My land which I have given you, and this house which I have consecrated for My name I will cast out of My sight and I will make it a proverb and a byword among all peoples. As for this house, which was exalted, everyone who passes by it will be astonished and say, 'Why has the Lord done thus to this land and to this house?' And they will say, 'Because they forsook the Lord, the God of their fathers who brought them from the land of Egypt, and they adopted other gods and worshiped them and served them; therefore He has brought all this adversity on them.'" (vv. 19–22)

Which hand would Solomon choose? One contained images of his sons and grandsons sitting on his throne in a never-ending line of godly kings. But as he peered into the other hand, darkness shrouded his view. He saw himself uprooted from his homeland, his golden temple crumbling and ridiculed, and his people suffering God's stern reproach. Which would be his destiny? It depended on one thing—his desire to walk with God.

Spiritual Survival: Then and Now

Although our situation differs from Solomon's in many ways—the United States is not Israel; we live under grace, not the Law; God's Spirit dwells within us rather than in a temple—the principles are the same. Like Israel, we have enjoyed God's blessings during our more than two hundred years of existence. Perhaps the reason relates, in part, to our original pattern and purpose for government having been based on biblical standards. However, it is clear that we have drifted from our former commitment to be "one nation under God." Could we be in danger of forfeiting God's blessing?

If God paid us a night visit, what counsel would He offer? Probably, it would be similar to the survival instructions He gave Solomon: humble ourselves, pray, seek His face, and turn from wickedness. There is healing in that simple message—healing for individuals, for families, for businesses, for nations. But the job can't be done by committee. It won't be accomplished in the paneled rooms on Capitol Hill, in judges' chambers, voting booths, city council meetings, or even church gatherings. It must be done individually, by "My people who are called by My name"—Christians—who unconditionally surrender their wills to God.

According to Peter Marshall and David Manuel, authors of *The Light and the Glory*, this approach puts

the responsibility directly upon each of us who has a personal relationship with our Saviour—much as we might like to blame the immorality of others for the precipitous rate of decline. But the responsibility is ours, and it always has been. When Solomon Stoddard once challenged Increase Mather on this very point, pointing out that the covenanted Christians in seventeenth-century New England were only a fraction of the population, Mather retorted that, nonetheless, that fraction was sufficient to "stand for the entire land" and "redeem the whole."[2]

We *can* make a difference! And praying humbly for our country and for ourselves is a good place to start.

2. Peter Marshall and David Manuel, *The Light and the Glory* (Old Tappan, N.J.: Fleming H. Revell Co., 1977), p. 356.

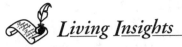 *Living Insights*

We began this chapter by asking, "What can we do for our country?" After studying God's counsel to Solomon, we realize now that the answer lies less in "doing" and more in "being." We may work feverishly to heal our country, but if our hearts are not right, true change will not take place. Recall the inner qualities God is looking for:

- The attitude of a servant

- A spirit of dependence

- A willingness to wait

- A response of obedience

It is sad that many Christians exhibit to the world just the opposite: an arrogant attitude, an independent spirit, an impatience to run ahead, and a do-my-own-thing response. With hearts like that, how can God hear our prayers? How can He forgive our sins? How can He heal our land?

For a few moments, let God's Spirit be a mirror of your own spirit. Ask Him to show you any sinful attitudes that might be inhibiting your prayers and limiting God's power in your world. Write down what you see.

_____

_____

_____

_____

Now follow the steps God gave Solomon: humble yourself before Him, pray for forgiveness, renew your desire to seek His face, and commit yourself to turn from any wicked ways.

_____

_____

_____

_____

Oh, our God, we are in desperate times.

Integrity is a forgotten word in business. Even our government has pockets of pollution that we continue to discover. You are the only source of true purity. You are the only hope, our future. Forgive us for our smug complacency, for once we find ourselves well-fed, who really could care less about the hungry? And once we are comfortably in from the rain, who could care about the shelter of another?

Begin by humbling us, our Father, giving us hearts of compassion . . . giving us a heart for those who do not have sufficient resources to survive. Open our ears to the cry of the hurting. May physicians practice a compassionate medical practice. May attorneys see and feel the hurt and the need of their clients. . . . May teachers teach for the sheer joy of stretching minds and developing a curious heart for the world that You have given us to enjoy. And may preachers preach the truth. . . . Father, purify us as a people. Do a deep, soul-searching work within our hearts and then within our homes, and then cause the salt and light to infect and impact others with truth—not so we will feel better, but so we will survive. We ask this in the strong name of Christ. Amen.[3]

Small Group Insights

1. How are the people in your church responding to the downward spiral of society?

_____

_____

_____

_____

3. Charles R. Swindoll, from the sermon "How to Help Our Nation Survive," given at the First Evangelical Free Church of Fullerton, California, July 4, 1982.

2. How can you guard yourself against the pride, sinfulness, and moral compromise you encounter in your everyday life?

_____

_____

_____

_____

3. List some specific ways you can pray for your church and your small group as you stand up for truth.

_____

_____

_____

_____

4. List some specific ways you can pray for our nation and its leaders to seek God and obtain healing.

_____

_____

_____

_____

Chapter 8

A PASSION THAT STAYS BALANCED

1 Corinthians 9:4–23

Passion. Just reading the word sparks a fire within us, but the idea isn't easy to define. According to the dictionary, passion has four synonyms: "fervor, ardor, enthusiasm, zeal"; and it has as one of its meanings "intense, driving, or overmastering feeling or conviction."[1] These come close to capturing its spirit; but we still have just the bones—the word needs flesh.

Jesus certainly comes to mind when we think of passion, but so does another person in the New Testament: the apostle Paul. He was a man with intense, driving convictions. His enemies would curse him, and he'd keep on preaching the Gospel. They would beat him and stone him nearly to death, and he'd dust himself off and take his message to the next town. He refused to run scared, to take it easy, or to play it safe. If the sun rose, he considered it God's green light to pursue his mission in life. As long as there was breath in his lungs, the name of Christ would be on his lips and the passion of God would throb in his heart.

Four particular periods in Paul's life, like four photos in an album, reveal the fire in this man's passionate spirit.

Four Brief Glimpses of Paul

The first photo captures Paul before his conversion, when he was still Saul of Tarsus, a member of the Sanhedrin and a well-educated and respected Pharisee. It reveals that even *while he was lost, he passionately pressed on in his mission.* Unfortunately, his "mission" was persecuting Christians. In his own words, he testified to his savage zeal:

> "So then, I thought to myself that I had to do many things hostile to the name of Jesus of Nazareth. And this is just what I did in Jerusalem; not only did I lock up many of the saints in prisons, having received authority from the chief priests, but also

1. *Merriam-Webster's Collegiate Dictionary*, 10th ed., see "passion."

when they were being put to death I cast my vote against them. And as I punished them often in all the synagogues, I tried to force them to blaspheme; and being furiously enraged at them, I kept pursuing them even to foreign cities." (Acts 26:9–11)

While en route to Damascus, Saul met the object of his wrath face-to-face. In this second photo, we see him blinded by a flash of light and struck down by a glorious vision of Christ. But notice his response: *As he was converted, he passionately submitted to Christ.* When he realized he was fighting against God, he put up no resistance to changing his ways. Later, after Ananias explained to him the Lord's will for his life, his blindness fell away and the eyes of his spirit were opened. *"Immediately,"* the Scripture says,

he began to proclaim Jesus in the synagogues, saying, "He is the Son of God." (9:20, emphasis added)

The next photograph pictures him in his role as missionary, for *once he was saved, he passionately pursued his calling.* Changing his name from Jewish Saul to Roman Paul, he broke out of the gates of Jewry and charged into an empire full of pagans needing Christ. All former prejudices were cast aside as he set a pace for cross-cultural missions that no one since has been able to match. Through his teaching and writing, he forged a theology of grace from the iron legalism of the old covenant. He was a skilled debater, an insightful thinker, and a loving parent to his family of newborn churches.

The fourth page of Paul's life reveals a photo of him in a Roman dungeon. His stooped body bears the scars of his sufferings, yet the fire in his heart still burns hot. For *when he was facing death, he passionately finished the journey.* In his final letter, he challenged Timothy to "preach the word" (2 Tim. 4:2). He asked for his books and parchments to keep his mind sharp and focused on Scripture (see v. 13). He was determined to cross the finish line with his head held high:

I have fought the good fight, I have finished the course, I have kept the faith. (v. 7)

What a remarkable man of passion, from start to finish!

It would be easy to think that a person of such intense conviction and single-minded determination would run over people in the quest for gold. But Paul balanced his passion with his willingness to make sacrifices and adapt to the lifestyles of the people around him. This ability flowed out of his philosophy of evangelism, which he expressed in 1 Corinthians 9.

Three Balanced Guidelines for Ministry

As God's spokesman, Paul had access to a storehouse of privileges. He had the "right to eat and drink" (v. 4)—that is, to enjoy daily provisions from those to whom he ministered. He had the right to have a wife and a family (v. 5). He had the "right to refrain from working" in jobs other than his ministry (v. 6). He had the right to receive a salary from those he served. For proof of this last benefit, he called on Moses for support:

> For it is written in the Law of Moses, "You shall not muzzle the ox while he is threshing." God is not concerned about oxen, is He? Or is He speaking altogether for our sake? Yes, for our sake it was written, because the plowman ought to plow in hope, and the thresher to thresh in hope of sharing the crops. If we sowed spiritual things in you, is it too much if we reap material things from you? (vv. 9–11)

After all, the priests serving the temple enjoyed the meat they sacrificed on the altar (v. 13). The Lord even

> directed those who proclaim the gospel to get their living from the gospel. (v. 14; see also Luke 10:7–8)

Yet Paul refused to help himself to the bounty, so that he would "cause no hindrance to the gospel of Christ" (1 Cor. 9:12). Why might receiving pay for ministry hinder the Gospel? Because the corruption and excesses in the prevailing religious establishment could taint the newly revealed truth, as William Barclay illustrates:

> While the ordinary Jewish family ate meat at the most once a week the priests suffered from an occupational disease consequent on eating too much meat. Their privileges, the luxury of their lives, their rapacity were notorious; Paul knew all about this. He knew how they used religion as a means to grow fat; and he was determined that he would go to the other extreme and take nothing. . . .
> In the last analysis one thing dominated his

conduct. He would do nothing that would bring discredit on the gospel or hinder it. Men judge a message by the life and character of the man who brings it; and Paul was determined that his hands would be clean. He would allow nothing in his life to contradict the message of his lips. Someone once said to a preacher, "I cannot hear what you say for listening to what you are." No one could ever say that to Paul.[2]

Today, with public opinion of ministers at a discouraging low, we especially need to follow Paul's example for a balanced ministry. In verses 19–23, three guidelines emerge.

Having Freedom without Abusing One's Rights

Paul relished the freedom God's grace offered him, yet he refused to turn that freedom into a license for abuse. He would rather offer the Gospel "without charge" if doing so opened the door for someone to receive Christ (v. 18).

> For though I am free from all men, I have made myself a slave to all, so that I may win more. (v. 19)

The driving force in Paul's life was his all-consuming desire to win the lost. In verses 20–22, he illustrates how far he would go to communicate the Gospel when around three groups of people: Jews, pagans, and the weak.

First, *when around Jews.*

> To the Jews I became as a Jew, so that I might win Jews; to those who are under the Law, as under the Law though not being myself under the Law, so that I might win those who are under the Law . . . (v. 20)

If anyone could understand the Jewish mind, it was Paul. He could walk into a Hebrew home and immediately fit in as one of the family. He knew their traditions, their liturgies, their ceremonies; he knew what to say and do to win their trust. If it meant saving Jews, he could live by the Law, but he always refused to live under the Law with regard to his own salvation.

---

2. William Barclay, *The Letters to the Corinthians*, rev. ed., The Daily Study Bible Series (Philadelphia, Pa.: Westminster Press, 1975), p. 81.

Second, *when around pagans*.

> . . . to those who are without law, as without law,
> though not being without the law of God but under
> the law of Christ, so that I might win those who are
> without law. (v. 21)

If a Gentile host served him a nonkosher meal, he could eat it
with gratitude. He could mingle with pagans without giving off a
"holier than thou" attitude. Yet he never allowed their libertine
lifestyle to corrupt his commitment to Christ's moral standards.
Third, *when around the weak*.

> To the weak I became weak, that I might win the
> weak; I have become all things to all men, so that
> I may by all means save some. (v. 22)

The weak are immature believers whose consciences are easily
bruised. As an apostle, Paul could have intimidated them or made
them feel foolish for asking simple questions. He could have bowled
them over with his zeal for Christ or paraded his liberty before they
had time to grasp the meaning of grace. Instead, out of love, he
used his freedom as an opportunity to serve the weak (see Gal. 5:13).

In each situation, Paul did whatever was necessary to communicate the Gospel. Yet he never lost his spiritual equilibrium. In
one hand, he cradled his freedom under God's grace; in the other,
he held the restraints of love. Together, the two principles kept him
balanced and focused on the needs of people.

Being Flexible without Compromising One's Morals

Another guideline we can take from Paul's example concerns
his ability to be flexible. He could get along well with all kinds of
people, whether they were stuffy legalists or earthy pagans. Instead
of forcing them into his world, he stepped into theirs. And he did
this without compromising his convictions.

Flexibility need not suggest hypocrisy or softening of standards. It
simply means that, as God's voice in the world, we are aware of those
who listen to our lives. We're in touch with their needs and interests.

When speaking to an athlete about the Gospel, try to think as
an athlete. When talking to a person in business, use business-
related illustrations. When conversing with homemakers, address
their concerns about rearing responsible children. Become a student
of non-Christians and the world they live in. And be willing to

flex on amoral issues so that you "will cause no hindrance to the gospel of Christ" (1 Cor. 9:12).

Standing Firm without Becoming Aloof and Unaccountable

The final guideline appears in verse 23:

> I do all things for the sake of the gospel, so that I may become a fellow partaker of it. (v. 23)

As flexible as Paul was, there was one thing about which he would never bend—the Gospel. Upon that ground, he stood firm. Yet he didn't put himself above his message. He wasn't merely a dispenser of the truth, he was a partaker of it too. He was accountable to the words he preached. The Gospel was his soul and substance—the hub around which all the spokes of his life turned.

To spread the message of Christ, he would "become all things to all" people and he would "do all things"—that he may "by all means save some" (vv. 22–23). Can you feel the passion in his words? He gave his "all . . . all . . . all . . . all" for the sake of *some*. To us, that much effort for a seemingly small amount of gain seems futile. For Paul, though, it was worth it all—even if just for one.

Two Basic Principles to Remember

As we draw our thoughts to a close, let's lift Paul out of the picture for a moment and paint ourselves into it. He modeled the principle that *those who are passionate about going to all ends to reach the lost must stay flexible*. Are you flexible? Are you able to set aside your differences with people in the world? Are you making an effort to stay in touch with those outside the family of God? We don't have to travel to a foreign country to find non-Christians. We rub shoulders with them every day—at the supermarket, at the Little League game, at the office. Step into their world, and let them see Christ in your life.

Second, Paul showed us that *those who are passionate about reaching the lost by all means must stay available*. Are you available? Is Christ the center of your life—the One in charge of your career, your home, and your relationships? Perhaps He is pointing you in a different direction, asking you to leave the familiar and step into the world of the non-Christian. Are you prepared to give your all to save some? Ask the Lord to ignite your heart with Paul's passion. And get ready for fireworks!

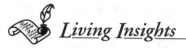 *Living Insights*

Imagine that your non-Christian neighbors invite you to a party. When you arrive, you immediately realize this is no church potluck. Strings of cigarette smoke wisp through the air. Everyone is cradling either a beer bottle or a wine glass in their hand. And the pulsating music and raucous laughter make conversing impossible without yelling.

What would be going through your mind during the evening? Would your eyes betray judgmental thoughts? Would you feel uneasy? Fearful?

_____

_____

What difficulties would you encounter as you tried to maintain your Christian standards during a party like this?

_____

_____

Jesus felt quite at home with worldly people, so much so that he was charged with being "a gluttonous man and a drunkard, a friend of tax collectors and sinners" (Matt. 11:19b). We would think, because of His unyielding holiness, that He wouldn't come near non-Christian gatherings. Yet, ironically, the Son of God was most comfortable around sinners.

Read Luke 5:29–32, and write down why He sought out the company of worldly people.

_____

_____

How can Jesus' example give you courage to be flexible around non-Christians without compromising your standards?

_____

_____

 *Small Group Insights*

1. What would you describe as your passions? How do they impact your spiritual life?

   _____

   _____

   _____

2. How do you balance your freedom through Christ with your love for the lost and hurting?

   _____

   _____

   _____

3. How flexible are you in reaching out to others to share the Gospel?

   _____

   _____

   _____

4. How available are you to meet the needs of those around you?

   _____

   _____

   _____

Chapter 9

CAN ONE PERSON
MAKE A DIFFERENCE?

Selected Scriptures

By now in our study, if you're like me, you want to believe that you can make a difference in the world, but a voice inside keeps protesting, "Be realistic! The river of history is too wide, and the current of evil is too strong. One person can't possibly change the course of the world."

A quick glance at the evening news seems to reinforce that message. Our inner cities have become war zones, our judicial system is a tangle of legal games, and our families are unraveling at the seams. It takes just one step into society's icy waters to feel sin's swift current. The idea of making a difference sounds nice, but for those trying to keep from drowning, is it possible?

From the vortex of pressing problems swirling around us, the task looks too difficult to even try. We need to get to high, dry ground, a place of perspective so we can see that our struggles are not unique but have occurred through the ages. And they've been squarely challenged by difference-making people. There we'll draw hope and strength from some of these individuals who did the impossible—who changed the direction of the world. So, if your seat belts are fastened, let's go!

Difference-Makers in History

Consider the many individuals from the worlds of religion, science, art, music, and literature who have impacted our lives and hearts . . . call to mind the inventors, explorers, statesmen, preachers, and military strategists. The list is pretty impressive, and this is only a small portion of it:

- Martin Luther, who sparked the Protestant Reformation

- Leonardo da Vinci, who opened the age of the Renaissance

- William Shakespeare, who was the playwright of the ages

- John Bunyan, who has guided the progress of millions of pilgrims

70

- Alexander Pope, whose intellectual investments still profit today's thinkers

- Benjamin Franklin, who invented bifocals

- Eli Whitney, who gave us the cotton gin

- Thomas Edison, who brought us out of darkness with electric light

- Henry Ford, whose Model T broadened borders to the butcher across town or the grandchildren across the country

Then there are the Beethovens, the Columbuses, the Lincolns. God's spurs to the nations—Jonathan Edwards, John Wesley, and Charles Spurgeon. Churchill and Gandhi, shaping the destiny of their countries and beyond. The discoveries of Curie, Einstein, Pasteur; the generals Montgomery and Eisenhower.

Where would we be today without these people who altered the stream of history?

Their stories prove that one person *can* make a difference. Yet the voice inside you is probably retorting, "These people were unusually talented. I'm no Einstein. I'm only an ordinary person. What can I do to make the world a better place?"

The good news is that you don't have to be an Einstein. The Scriptures show us that God uses ordinary individuals—and very often uses them individually—to do extraordinary things. See for yourself!

Difference-Makers in the Bible

Many times, God *prefers* to use only one person. For example, during the days of Ezekiel, corrupt religious and political leaders were extorting money, profaning God's sacred things, and "destroying lives in order to get dishonest gain" (Ezek. 22:25–27). Israel had become a nation of liars, oppressors, and thieves, who took advantage of the poor and "oppressed the sojourner without justice" (v. 29). What plan did the Lord have in mind for rescuing His people from sin's murky depths?

> "I searched for a man among them who would build up the wall and stand in the gap before Me for the land, so that I would not destroy it; but I found no one." (v. 30)

He wasn't searching for a committee or a group of legislators. To spare Israel from destruction, all He needed was *one* person willing to stand for what was right.

Only rarely does God intervene directly in history, such as the time He confused the languages at the Tower of Babel or rained down judgment on Sodom and Gomorrah. Instead, His *modus operandi* is to use individuals—people like us—to stem the tide of wickedness and chart new paths toward godliness.

Let's take a look at some of those ordinary people God used— people who "stood in the gap" and made a difference in their world.

Noah

Israel's wickedness pales in comparison to the evil in the world during the days of Noah. According to Genesis 6:5, "Every intent of the thoughts of [humankind's] heart was only evil *continually*" (emphasis added). Because immorality was so pervasive, "the Lord was sorry that He had made man on the earth, and He was grieved in His heart" (v. 6).

So the Lord decided to flood the earth and destroy every living thing. Only "Noah found favor in the eyes of the Lord" (v. 8). Without his faithfulness to God and willingness to build the ark, none of us would be here today.

Abraham

After the Flood, the population grew and nations were formed. God wanted a people all His own to be a model of His mercy and a channel for His grace. Searching the world, he found just the man to father such a nation—Abraham, the one through whom "all the families of the earth will be blessed" (Gen. 12:3b).

Joseph

Abraham's grandson, Jacob, had twelve sons whose descendants would later head the twelve tribes of Israel. One son, Joseph, was especially favored by his father. So his jealous brothers dumped him in a pit and sold him to slave traders. He wound up in Egypt, where he was falsely accused and thrown into a dungeon. "What good could come out of my life?" he must have wondered. Still, he remained faithful to the Lord, and God elevated him from the prison to the palace as the prime minister of Egypt—a position he would use to save his family from famine and keep the dream of God's people alive. Later he was able to say to his forgiven brothers, "You meant evil against me, but God meant it for good in order to . . . preserve many people alive" (Gen. 50:20).

Moses

As the years passed, subsequent Pharaohs forgot Joseph and his favorable stance toward the Hebrews. The new regimes enslaved the people, beating them with the whips of oppression and hatred. Would God's plan for His people end here, in the mud pits of Goshen? No, God had selected a baby named Moses, whom Pharaoh's daughter drew out of the Nile and brought up as her own. For forty years, he was a prince; then, forced out of Egypt for another forty years, a humble shepherd. But at age eighty, God chose him to become the deliverer of the Hebrews.

Joshua

Upon Moses' death, Joshua took over as the general to lead the Hebrews in their conquest of Canaan. The Lord reassured Joshua that Moses' torch of divine strength was now his to carry.

> "No man will be able to stand before you all the days of your life. Just as I have been with Moses, I will be with you; I will not fail you or forsake you." (Josh. 1:5)

When God uses individuals, He doesn't leave them alone to perform their difficult tasks. He's the strength in their arms and the voice on their lips. If God is in it, anything is possible!

The Judges

Under Joshua's command, the promise of land for the Hebrews became reality. But over time, a new enemy—affluence—invaded the people's hearts, and the nation became increasingly indifferent toward God's laws. What strategy would the Lord employ to recapture Israel's affections? First, He gave them into the hands of their enemies. Then, when they came to their senses and repented, He raised up individual judges—such as Deborah, Gideon, Jephthah, and Samson—to deliver them.

Samuel

Samuel ministered as a judge and prophet during a unique period of transition in Israel's history when the twelve autonomous tribes unified under a central government. With one hand toward heaven and the other stretched out to the people, Samuel stood in the gap between God and Israel, guiding the nation through this turbulent time. He was also the one to crown Israel's first king, Saul.

Saul, David, and Solomon

Saul mounted the throne as the nation's first king, then came David and his son Solomon. During each of their reigns, they were the principal difference-makers in the land—sometimes impacting the nation for good; sometimes, for bad. But overall, their reigns comprised the golden era of Israel's united, burgeoning kingdom.

The Prophets

After Solomon died, animosity between the northern and southern tribes forced a civil war. As a result, ten tribes in the North seceded to form their own monarchy, initiating what has been called the divided kingdom period. Once more, God's plan for His people included enlisting individuals to confront the nations with His truth and model obedience to His words. The books in the Bible starting with Isaiah and ending with Malachi roll-call most of their names.

Ezra and Nehemiah

Despite God's warnings, both kingdoms fell to invaders. The Assyrians conquered the northern kingdom, and the Babylonians crushed the southern. After a time in captivity, Zerubbabel, Ezra, and Nehemiah led the Jews home to Jerusalem in three expeditions. These men had the vision and faith to rebuild the temple, the city walls, and, most importantly, the spirit of the people.

John the Baptizer

During the four-hundred-year gap between the Old and New Testaments, no prophets appeared on the biblical horizon until John the Baptizer stormed in from the wilderness, raising dust clouds among the religious elite and preparing the way for the Messiah.

Jesus Christ

More than any other, the life of Jesus Christ epitomizes the power of one person to change lives. Philip Schaff describes eloquently the difference Jesus has made in history:

> This Jesus of Nazareth, without money and arms, conquered more millions than Alexander, Caesar,

Mohammed, and Napoleon; without science and learning, He shed more light on things human and divine than all philosophers and scholars combined; without the eloquence of schools, He spoke such words of life as were never spoken before or since and produced effects which lie beyond the reach of orator or poet; without writing a single line, He set more pens in motion, and furnished themes for more sermons, orations, discussions, learned volumes, works of art, and songs of praise, than the whole army of great men of ancient and modern times.[1]

Peter, Stephen, and Paul

Jesus made scores of others into difference-makers, who then flowed into the world like ripples in a pond. Three of the earliest were Peter, the disciple who denied Christ but later became His chief spokesman; Stephen, the first person in the Bible to be martyred for his faith; and Paul, the former persecutor of Christians who became the early church's greatest champion of the Gospel.

Can One Person Make a Difference?

Our tour through secular and biblical history brings us full circle to our original question. Based on the precedent of the past, the answer is an overwhelming yes! One person *can* change the world—in fact, this is the way God works. He's still searching for that one man or woman "whose heart is completely His" whom He can use to achieve His purposes (2 Chron. 16:9).

Is your heart completely His? That is the most important question. Who knows what new vistas God has in mind for your era. If your heart is His, you can take part in His vision. With Him, you can make all the difference in the world.

---

1. Philip Schaff, *The Person of Christ* (New York, N.Y.: American Tract Society, 1913), p. 33; as quoted by Josh McDowell in *Evidence That Demands a Verdict*, rev. ed. (San Bernardino, Calif.: Here's Life Publishers, 1979), vol. 1, p. 132.

🎵 Living Insights

In the late 1980s and early 1990s, the world watched in amazement as a wildfire of change swept across Eastern Europe. According to author Michael Green, among the many causes of the blaze was the undeniable influence of Jesus Christ in the lives of the common people.

> In Russia, religious faith has survived nearly seventy years of determined assault by militant atheism and now numbers at least sixty million Christians, many of whom, like Alexander Solzhenitsyn, have been tempered by imprisonment in gulags and mental hospitals for their beliefs. Such people have been at the heart of the reform movement that has eventually flowered in perestroika and glasnost. In Poland, Solidarity began, and largely continues, as a nonviolent Christian rebellion against an authoritarianism that crippled the human spirit. It is around the church that popular support has rallied in the independence movements of Lithuania, Latvia, and Georgia; and it is the church that has sustained their spirits amid the sea of atheism and political oppression. It was a Romanian pastor who ignited the flame of his country's uprising against the dictator's ruthless regime. The prayer meetings in Leipzig lighted the fuse that exploded in East Germany's peaceful revolution. We could not ask for clearer evidence of the impact of Jesus. That one solitary life continues to have an unparalleled impact on human affairs.[2]

One Lord, one pastor, one prayer meeting, one church, one movement. One by one, heart by heart, a difference was made in what seemed an impossible situation.

You may not live behind the walls of a totalitarian government, but perhaps you face an obstacle to truth and righteousness in your workplace or school or neighborhood. If so, begin making a difference

---

2. Michael Green, *Who Is This Jesus?* (Nashville, Tenn.: Thomas Nelson Publishers, Oliver Nelson, 1992), p. 3.

in that situation at the same place the believers in Europe began: Jesus Christ. As Jesus said,

> "I am the vine, you are the branches; he who abides in Me and I in him, he bears much fruit, for apart from Me you can do nothing." (John 15:5)

In your efforts to make a difference, how are you reflecting Christ, His ideals of grace and truth and His glory?

_____

_____

_____

What does it mean to "abide in" Christ? What steps do you need to take to abide more deeply in Him?

_____

_____

_____

May Jesus' example and that of those believers in Eastern Europe inspire you to bear the ridicule and persecution that may come as you strive to change your world.

Small Group Insights

1. Besides those mentioned in this chapter, name some difference-makers in your life.

_____

_____

_____

2. What did these people say and do that had such a tremendous impact on your life?

_____

_____

_____

_____

_____

_____

_____

3. What spheres of influence are you operating in right now (for example, your small group, your church, your family, your group of friends, your school, your workplace)?

_____

_____

_____

_____

_____

_____

_____

4. How can you follow the example of your heroes by impacting those in your spheres of influence? List some practical ways you can make a difference.

_____

_____

_____

_____

_____

_____

_____

Chapter 10
THIS IS NO TIME FOR WIMPS!
1 Corinthians 15:58; Hebrews 11:23–27

Most Americans who lived during the Second World War can still remember sitting beside the radio with family members, listening with rapt attention to the voice of a statesman with a British accent who did not know the meaning of the word *surrender*.

Winston Churchill's first statement as prime minister to the House of Commons, May 13, 1940, was this: "I have nothing to offer but blood, toil, tears and sweat."[1]

Three weeks later, after the capture of Dunkirk, Churchill rallied the nation with these words:

> "We shall not flag or fail. We shall go on to the end.
> We shall fight in France, we shall fight on the seas
> and oceans, we shall fight with growing confidence
> and growing strength in the air, we shall defend our
> island, whatever the cost may be, we shall fight on
> the beaches, we shall fight on the landing grounds,
> we shall fight in the fields and in the streets, we shall
> fight in the hills; we shall never surrender."[2]

Five months later, reporting on the war situation to the House of Commons, Churchill said,

> "Death and sorrow will be the companions of our
> journey; hardship our garment; constancy and valor
> our only shield. We must be united, we must be
> undaunted, we must be inflexible."[3]

In a unique speech to the London County Council, July 14, 1941, he referred to "a comradeship of suffering, of endurance" and told Hitler and his Nazi forces: "We will have no truce or parley with you, or the grisly gang who work your wicked will. You do your worst—and we will do our best." And later, "We shall never

---

1. Winston Churchill, as quoted in *Bartlett's Familiar Quotations*, 15th ed., rev. and enl., ed. Emily Morison Beck (Boston, Mass.: Little, Brown and Co., 1980), p. 743.

2. Churchill, in *Bartlett's*, p. 744.

3. Churchill, in *Bartlett's*, p. 744.

turn from our purpose, however sombre the road, however grievous the cost."[4]

He stirred the boys of Harrow School that same year on October 29:

> "Do not let us speak of darker days; let us speak rather of sterner days. These are not dark days: these are great days—the greatest days our country has ever lived; and we must all thank God that we have been allowed, each of us according to our stations, to play a part in making these days memorable in the history of our race."[5]

And one more—"'Not in vain' may be the pride of those who survived and the epitaph of those who fell."[6]

Those were hard times. Determined times. Disciplined times. Patriotic times. Such harsh times spawned men and women of character who understood the words Churchill used—*constancy, determination, faithfulness, durability* . . . no matter the sacrifice or cost.

"Not in vain." As Churchill's words ring in our ears, we find that they actually echo what the apostle Paul wrote nineteen centuries earlier.

> Therefore, my beloved brethren, be steadfast, immovable, always abounding in the work of the Lord, knowing that your toil is not in vain in the Lord. (1 Cor. 15:58)

Or as the Living Bible puts it, "Nothing you do for the Lord is ever wasted."

As believers today, we must renew that same spirit of determination and commitment to faithfulness, to constancy, to endurance—no matter how somber the road or how grievous the cost. We must restore the passion of Paul as we march into the twenty-first century "steadfast, immovable, always abounding in the work of the Lord." This means not caving in; not capitulating morally, financially, or ethically; not giving up; not compromising on our theology; not ignoring the needs around us; and not conducting ourselves in arrogance or lacking in compassion.

---

4. Sir Winston Churchill, *Great War Speeches*, comp. Charles Eade (1957; reprint, London, England: Transworld Publishers, Corgi Books, 1965), pp. 128, 129, 130.

5. Churchill, in *Bartlett's*, p. 745.

6. Churchill, in *Bartlett's*, p. 746.

"Not failure," said the poet, "but low aim, is crime."[7] And so the challenge before us is to aim high, stand tall, be models of integrity and vision and responsibility and purity. Most of us are able to handle greater challenges than we ever place before ourselves. Our problem, which can become our peril, lies not in raising our sights too high, but in setting our aim too low.

During his difficult years in the White House, our sixteenth president would occasionally slip into the midweek service of the New York Presbyterian Church, pastored by a Dr. Gurley. Lincoln went there to find strength and solace in the midst of the pressures of the Civil War. In order not to distract the congregation, he would listen from the privacy of the pastor's study, which was built adjoining the sanctuary off to the side.

A young aide always accompanied Lincoln on this journey. After one particular meeting, the aide asked him what he thought of the sermon that night. "I thought it was well thought through, powerfully delivered, and very eloquent." "Then you thought it was a great sermon?" the young man asked. "No," said the president, "it failed. It failed because Dr. Gurley did not ask us to do something great."[8]

Perhaps that is why Churchill's words have outlived him. Perhaps that explains why Paul's words continue to stir us and motivate us nineteen centuries after he wrote them. True challenges force us out of our comfort zones and dare us to reach beyond the familiar.

In the words of the late, great preacher John Henry Jowett, "Ministry that costs nothing, accomplishes nothing."[9] That explains why all of us long to hear a fresh word from God; for when God speaks He never aims low. He expects great things. He asks great things.

When the Lord spoke to Noah, who stood alone in a decadent generation, He said to him, "Build an ark." When He spoke to Joseph, He said, "Return good for evil. Forgive your brothers." When He spoke to Moses over the howling winds of the desert, He said to him, "Lead My people out of Egypt." When He spoke to David, He said, unequivocally, "Kill the giant." When He spoke to Isaiah,

7. James Russell Lowell, as quoted in *Illustrations Unlimited*, ed. James S. Hewett (Wheaton, Ill.: Tyndale House Publishers, 1988), p. 459.

8. Adapted from Bruce Larson's *What God Wants to Know* (San Francisco, Calif.: HarperSanFrancisco, 1993), pp. 46–47.

9. John Henry Jowett, as quoted by Warren W. Wiersbe and David Wiersbe in *Making Sense of the Ministry* (1983; reprint, Grand Rapids, Mich.: Baker Book House, 1989), p. 36.

He said, "Who will go? Whom shall I send?" When He got the attention of Peter, after the big fisherman had fallen and failed, He said to him, "Feed My sheep." When the Apostle of Grace stood on the westernmost shores of Turkey, wondering what God wanted, He said to him, "Come over to Europe and help us."

God asks something great of every one of us. Not something easy. Not something that comes naturally or something that will cost us nothing. But something great so that we, too, may join the ranks of those in God's Hall of Faith (see Heb. 11).

The years before us will become increasingly difficult years in which to minister. Count on it. The church will deal with issues no one could have imagined fifty years ago. Count on it. Every ministry will have its mettle tested, and we will face trials and temptations like never before. Our plate of challenges will continue to be full. Count on it.

The demands on God's servants have never been more intense. In the heat of the battle, it's easy to forget that our God will fight for us. Under the cynical eye of critics and haters of God, we may be tempted to throw a pity party, to lick our wounds and sing in harmony with Elijah, "I alone am left. I'm the only one who stands by the truth. Woe is me! Woe is me! I think I'll eat some worms!"

When you hit those times of feeling sorry for yourself and giving up—just as we all do—let Oswald Chambers' words give you a hand up:

> If you are devoted to the cause of humanity, you will soon be exhausted and have your heart broken by ingratitude, but if the mainspring of your service is love for Jesus, you can serve men although they treat you as a door-mat. Never look for justice in this world, but never cease to give it.[10]

Tucked away in Hebrews 11 is the minibiography of a man whose character and mainspring of service can show us how to aim for greatness.

> By faith Moses, when he was born, was hidden
> for three months by his parents, because they saw

---

10. Oswald Chambers, as quoted in *Oswald Chambers: The Best from All His Books*, comp. and ed. Harry Verploegh (Nashville, Tenn.: Thomas Nelson Publishers, Oliver Nelson, 1987), p. 320.

he was a beautiful child; and they were not afraid of the king's edict. (v. 23)

Isn't it easy to be afraid of the people around us? We're often intimidated by what others will think of us, say to us, or do to us—and what *we think* they might think, say, or do—that we, in effect, ascribe mythical superpowers to them that they can't possibly possess. They are merely fellow humans with their own sets of weaknesses, just as we are. Moses' parents took the first steps in instilling greatness in their son by modeling courage—a trait that would come to shape Moses' own life.

> By faith Moses, when he had grown up, refused to be called the son of Pharaoh's daughter, choosing rather to endure ill-treatment with the people of God than to enjoy the passing pleasures of sin, considering the reproach of Christ greater riches than the treasures of Egypt; for he was looking to the reward. By faith he left Egypt, not fearing the wrath of the king; for *he endured, as seeing Him who is unseen.* (vv. 24–27, emphasis added)

These last few words hold the key to greatness: Because Moses' eyes were on God, he was able to endure. The Living Bible says he "kept right on going." The New International Version, "He persevered." The New English, "He was resolute." The Amplified, "[He] held staunchly to his purpose." Moffatt's quaint rendering, "He never flinched."

Moses had staying power. He kept his eyes on the goal and not on the obstacles. He endured in his eighties, in his nineties, well past his one-hundredth birthday. He endured despite the contempt of Pharaoh. He endured the stubbornness of the Hebrews, who grumbled, maligned, complained, and rebelled. He endured amidst the criticism of those closest to him—Miriam, his sister; Aaron, his brother; Dathan and Abiram, his companions. He endured despite being disappointed at the spies who returned more impressed with the odds against them than with the God who was for them.

"He endured." How? "As seeing Him who is unseen." He fixed his eyes on his invisible Lord and never looked back.

On the basis of Moses' example, the challenge for every one of us is to endure, to stand firm, to be steadfast, to model faithfulness:

• Even when conspirators seem to prosper.

- Even when the wicked seem to be winning.
- Even when the pressure seems unbearable.
- Even when the critics won't keep quiet.
- Even when big people act contemptibly small.
- Even when you feel as though you're all alone.
- Even when wrong is enthroned and truth is fighting for existence.

Whatever you are facing as you stand on the edge of a new commitment, stand strong. Walk in quiet confidence, not veiled pride. Be firm without being unteachable and stubborn. Be enduring but not discourteous. Be full of truth, balanced well with grace.

What promise is ours for enduring? We have a threefold expectation: (1) In life, to borrow from Churchill, "I have nothing to offer but blood, toil, tears and sweat." (2) In death, to borrow from Paul, three words, "Not in vain." (3) But in heaven, to borrow from the One who came to seek and to save that which was lost, "Well done, good and faithful servant."

 Living Insights

While Paul challenges us to be steadfast and immovable, James addresses the flip side and warns us of the dangers of doubting:

> . . . the one who doubts is like the surf of the sea, driven and tossed by the wind. For that man ought not to expect that he will receive anything from the Lord, being a double-minded man, unstable in all his ways. (James 1:6b–8)

Do you sometimes feel as though you're riding waves of doubt? When things are going well—your bank account is brimming with reserves, currents of love are flowing between your family members, and a cool breeze of security is comforting your spirit—the ocean of life swells under you. You're riding high! Trusting the Lord comes easy, as well as praying, giving of yourself, and resisting temptation.

Then, suddenly, the wave breaks, and everything comes crashing down in a spray of white foam. Unexpected bills surface, relationships become choppy, and problems jut up like coral reefs from the ocean floor of your life.

When that happens, is it difficult for you to remain steadfast and immovable? Does your faith go crashing down along with everything else? Does your commitment to obey Christ get lost in the surging surf?

If you tend to be "driven and tossed by the wind," describe how that tendency evidences itself in your life.

_____

_____

_____

Moses endured because he kept his eyes on "Him who is unseen"—Christ (Heb. 11:27b). How can keeping your eyes on your circumstances instead of on Christ make you more vulnerable to the waves of doubt (see also Matt. 14:22–33)?

_____

_____

_____

First Corinthians 15:50–57 provides the basis of Paul's promise that our "toil is not in vain in the Lord" (v. 58b). Take a moment to read these verses. How can focusing on your future with Christ help you remain steadfast and immovable today?

_____

_____

_____

One final thought. As you step into battle, the odds may seem against you and the task overwhelming. At times, you are bound to feel weak, doubtful, and lonely. Remember this prayer by Martin Luther—the difference-maker with whom we began our study and with whom we will close. Let his expression of surrender guide you to his secret source of strength.

> *Behold, Lord, an empty vessel that needs to be filled.*
> *My Lord, fill it. I am weak in the faith; strengthen me.*
> *I am cold in love; warm me and make me fervent, that*
> *my love may go out to my neighbor. I do not have a*

strong and firm faith; at times I doubt and am unable to trust you altogether. O Lord, help me. Strengthen my faith and trust in you. In you I have sealed the treasure of all I have. I am poor; you are rich and came to be merciful to the poor. I am a sinner; you are upright. With me, there is an abundance of sin; in you is the fullness of righteousness. Therefore I will remain with you, of whom I can receive, but to whom I may not give. [11]

 ## Small Group Insights

1. From your study in this guide, what would you say are the most vital qualities of a difference-maker?

   _____

   _____

   _____

   _____

2. What challenges do difference-makers face?

   _____

   _____

   _____

   _____

3. Name one challenge you are facing in your life right now. How can you demonstrate the principles you have learned as you deal with this situation?

   _____

   _____

   _____

   _____

11. Martin Luther, as quoted in *The One Year Book of Personal Prayer* (Wheaton, Ill.: Tyndale House Publishers, 1991), p. 8.

BOOKS FOR
PROBING FURTHER

Dates are hard to remember, aren't they? That's why we invent ditties, like, "In fourteen-hundred-ninety-two, Columbus sailed the ocean blue." Here's one to help you recall the birth of the Reformation: "In fifteen-hundred-seventeen, Luther stood on Halloween." OK, OK, it's kind of silly. But it may prod you to remember that on October 31, 1517, Martin Luther posted his Ninety-five Theses, protesting certain abuses within the Roman church. Although Luther's stand was only a single flame in an era of darkness, it ignited a blaze that still burns in the heart of every Christian who holds fast to the Reformation anthem: *sola fide*, "faith alone."

You don't have to do something big to make a difference in the world. One simple truth struck against the flint of real life can be enough to light a bonfire of change.

Mothers Against Drunk Drivers (MADD) grew out of one mother's determination to rid the highways of drunk drivers. The Promise Keepers movement arose from one man's conviction that Christian men should help each other maintain their integrity.

Could God be giving you a vision for making your world a better place? The dream must come from Him, but we can help you get started. The following list of books will explain more about becoming a difference-maker. Who knows what reformations the Lord may spark through you?

Aldrich, Joe. *Prayer Summits: Seeking God's Agenda for Your Community.* Portland, Oreg.: Multnomah Press, 1992.

Anderson, Leith. *A Church for the 21st Century.* Minneapolis, Minn.: Bethany House Publishers, 1992.

Bainton, Roland H. *Here I Stand: A Life of Martin Luther.* New York, N.Y.: Abingdon-Cokesbury Press, 1950.

Barna, George. *The Power of Vision.* Ventura, Calif.: Gospel Light, Regal Books, 1992.

―――. *Turning Vision into Action.* Ventura, Calif.: Regal Books, 1997.

Collins, Gary R. *You Can Make a Difference*. Grand Rapids, Mich.: Zondervan Publishing House, 1992.

Colson, Charles. *Faith on the Line: Dare to Make a Kingdom Difference*. Wheaton, Ill.: Scripture Press Publications, Victor Books, 1994.

Colson, Charles, with Ellen Santilli Vaughn. *The Body: Being Light in the Darkness*. Dallas, Tex.: Word Publishing, 1992.

Ingram, Chip. *Holy Ambition: What It Takes to Make a Difference for God*. Chicago, Ill.: Moody Press, 2002.

Kent, Carol. *Becoming a Woman of Influence: Making a Lasting Impact on Others*. Colorado Springs, Colo.: NavPress, 1999.

Maxwell, John C. *Becoming a Person of Influence*. Nashville, Tenn.: Thomas Nelson Publishers, 1997.

Pollock, John. *The Apostle: A Life of Paul*. Wheaton, Ill.: Scripture Press Publications, Victor Books, 1985.

Spader, Dann, and Gary Mayes. *Growing a Healthy Church*. Chicago, Ill.: Moody Press, 1991.

Stott, John R.W. *Involvement: Being a Responsible Christian in a Non-Christian Society*. Old Tappan, N.J.: Fleming H. Revell Co., 1985.

Swindoll, Charles R. *Living Above the Level of Mediocrity: A Commitment to Excellence*. Dallas, Tex.: Word Publishing, 1989.

Waitley, Denis. *Seeds of Greatness*. Old Tappan, N.J.: Fleming H. Revell Co., 1983.

Some of the books listed may be out of print and available only through a library. For those currently available, please contact your local Christian bookstore. Books by Charles R. Swindoll are available through Insight for Living. IFL also offers some books by other authors—please note the ordering information that follows and contact the office that serves you.

NOTES

NOTES

NOTES

NOTES

ORDERING INFORMATION

CAN ONE PERSON MAKE A DIFFERENCE?

If you would like to order additional Bible study guides, purchase the audio series that accompanies this guide, or request our product catalogs, please contact the office that serves you.

United States and International Locations:
Insight for Living
Post Office Box 269000
Plano, TX 75026-9000

1-800-772-8888, 24 hours a day, seven days a week (U.S. contacts) International constituents may contact the U.S. office through mail queries.

Canada:
Insight for Living Ministries
Post Office Box 2510
Vancouver, BC V6B 3W7

1-800-663-7639, 24 hours a day, seven days a week
info@insightcanada.org

Australia:
Insight for Living, Inc.
20 Albert Street
Blackburn, VIC 3130, Australia

Toll-free 1800 772 888 or (03) 9877-4277, 9:00 A.M. to 5:00 P.M., Monday through Friday
insight.aus@insight.org

Internet:
www.insight.org

Bible Study Guide Subscription Program
Bible study guide subscriptions are available. Please call or write the office nearest you to find out how you can receive our Bible study guides on a regular basis.